The Wealth Increaser

I0161459

Successfully Building Wealth Yourself is Now Possible

Learn How to Build Wealth in a Stress-Free Manner

Thomas (TJ) Underwood

The Wealth Increaser

Library of Congress Cataloging-in-Publication Data

Copyright© 2014, 2023 by Thomas (TJ) Underwood

The Wealth Increaser: A concise and to the point guide on how you can successfully manage your finances yourself in any economic environment and achieve the goals that you desire most in a more efficient and effective manner.

Printed in the United States of America
Self-Published

Text design by Thomas (TJ) Underwood

ISBN: **978-1-953994-12-7**

Contents

The Wealth Increaser

Copyright© 2014, 2023 by Thomas (TJ) Underwood

Copyright® 2014, 2023 by Thomas (TJ) Underwood

All rights reserved. No part of this publication may be reproduced, stored in a retrieval system, or transmitted in any form by any means—electronic, mechanical, photocopy, recording, or any other—except for brief quotations in printed reviews, without prior permission of Thomas (TJ) Underwood.

You can e-mail him at tj@TheWealthIncreaser.com

Introduction

The Wealth Increaser®

It is important that you realize that many of our past successful and very successful client's take a long-term view toward achieving meaningful and significant goals—or achieving the major success that they desire!

It is important that you approach your credit and finances with the mindset that you will utilize the time that you have available appropriately and reflect on where you now are currently at with your credit and finances.

By doing so you can move forward effectively and efficiently, and you can further gain the mindset that you will learn consistently. And most importantly you can form a vision of your future that will provide you the ability to take the necessary action at the time when it is best to do so!

Your big-picture viewing of your future must be one where success in increasing your wealth to the level that you desire is the ultimate outcome. Although there may be roadblocks and obstacles along the way—success must constantly be on your radar!

Even though there may be delays, you must expect success and you must know that success will occur in your future.

You are the only person who can stand between your life purpose and achieving your life purpose!

When God has a plan for your life, the ability to achieve your life purpose is already within you—and you are the only person stopping your dreams from coming true!

It is important that you take the right action daily, yet still maintain the patience that is necessary to reach your goal(s) or life purpose.

You cannot mistake the fact that what you desire is not happening—or not happening fast enough to your liking—as a sign that it won't happen!

Quite the contrary, you must know that the success that you desire lies in the horizon because you have made the decision to press on and never quit, and you have come to that decision in a sincere manner!

You must also realize that the timing to do anything meaningful and significant in your life will never be just right. The proper time for you to act is right now! By doing so you can get positive momentum going in your life—today!

You must realize that happiness and joy comes from within you and the qualities that you need to attain success and attain happiness, joy and a constant feel-good vibe is already within you. However, you may need to approach your situation in a new or different manner to bring it all out!

You have unique abilities and experiences in your life that can truly be of benefit to others if you package what you know and present it in the appropriate manner.

Believe it or not—you have skills, talents, and abilities within you that you may not now realize that you have, and if you tap into your mind and heart at a deeper level—your gifts and talents will surely surface!

In the same spirit that our websites and debut book has changed the credit and financial habits of consumers worldwide for the better—so too will this book help you attain a very high level of success in increasing your future net worth by providing you the essential tools that you need to succeed!

Do you know that goal setting without a plan of action is basically just wishful thinking?

Do you know that **increasing your wealth** (or attaining any major goal) requires adequate planning and implementation?

You must ask yourself, are you the type who would prefer short-term gain or do you prefer benefiting for the long-term?

It is important that when you act towards increasing your wealth, you do what needs to be done the right way so that you can improve your **pathway to success** in your life.

You must be constantly aware that those who want you to achieve success the wrong way are really an enemy to your real success!

If you work on what God called you to do, you can attain your life purpose so that what you achieve can live for future generations.

You must realize that there are many who do good works throughout their lives. However, very few do what they were called to do!

Which one are you?

Do you know your original unique purpose for your life or are you following behind the paths of others or trying to duplicate what others have done or are doing?

You cannot follow the same beaten path as others as you are a unique creation, and you must pursue your unique path to the success that you desire—in all areas of your life!

You can simultaneously do good works and live in your life purpose.

Are you now doing or producing anything meaningful? Will what you are doing now outlive you—or will it wither away?

By being original in your approach to the success that you desire, you can leave something meaningful behind and live in your life purpose!

Why gripe and complain when you could be using that energy to look within and make the decision to find your purpose for your life?

When you sincerely do so, something will come alive within you that will provide you the power to make your dreams come true!

By doing so, outside forces will not have a negative effect on you because you will be going after what you desire with so much focus and determination that success CAN only be the ultimate outcome. You must make the decision to **C**ontrol your **A**ctions **N**ow!

Did you know that you have authority or control over the decisions that affect you and your family?

How are you going to live your present and future now that you know—or will soon know of powerful systems and approaches that can effectively put you and your family on a path to major success?

It is important that you analyze what your mind comes across in this book in an analytical, accurate, careful, and critical manner—and if you come across anything that "really speaks to you" and your situation, you must look even deeper into the subject matter!

You have the capacity to do and achieve more right now—right where you are!

The ability to excel was built inside of you early in your life and now is the time that you operate in excellence and **build your wealth** in an empowering manner!

In the rest of this Introduction, we will go over the "Life Stages of Financial Planning" to give you a conceptual overview of what you will need to do at various points in your life to increase your wealth in an intelligent, consistent, and proactive manner so that the stage for your successful building of wealth from this day forward can be set—so that your most pressing goals and dreams will become a reality.

Life Stages & Financial Planning

1) Formative & Young Adult Phase

2) Asset Accumulation Phase

3) Conservation/Protection Phase

4) Distribution/Gifting Phase

We realize that financial planning is often looked at as being a difficult process for some. However, the process is not as complex as you might think.

It is not uncommon for you to feel that you can't reach many of your financial goals and objectives, however with a **solid blueprint** of how successful financial planning is done, you too can succeed in reaching your financial planning **goals and objectives.**

By not putting together a solid financial plan to help you reach your and your family's goal(s), you may miss the opportunity to do the things in life that you and your family enjoy and miss the opportunity to pass on generational wealth.

By gaining a keen understanding of the life stages of financial planning and formulating goals you can put yourself and your family in a winning financial position. You can then put yourself in position to possibly reach all of the goals and objectives that you desire for yourself and your family.

Your key to building wealth is to process the information that you need in a format that you can understand so that you and your family can **meet your monthly expenses** and have **discretionary income** left over for additional savings, take that vacation that you and your family know you deserve, retire in a manner where you can do what you desire, leave a legacy for your heirs—or attain any other goal that you and your family may have.

Below we will go over various potential or actual stages in your financial life to help you get a conceptual understanding of the process of financial planning.

You can then put yourself in position to apply financial advice in a manner that will benefit you and your family the most!

1) *Formative & Young Adult Stage*

The Formative & Young Adult stage begins at birth and continues until your early twenties.

It starts with the financial education that you get from family, friends, and the larger environment that you grow up and live in.

In the formative and young adult phase you may have just begun working and you may not have a deep understanding about financial planning and goal setting, or finance in general and that may lead to some confusion for some.

Although the formative years are not cited by many economist and financial planners as a life cycle stage or phase, the formative years are often the most crucial.

It is the stage when you are open to learning good money management habits and establishing goals and objectives that are more attainable due to the longer time horizon for investing and savings in general.

If you were fortunate enough to have parents with high discretionary income and they were able to set up an investment and education funding plan after your birth or during your childhood years—you would have an advantage over those who did not have this benefit.

In addition, if you began working early as a teen and started contributing to a savings plan such as an IRA or other savings tool, you too would be in a better financial position than others at this same stage.

Also, if you were able to graduate from college, obtain a job early and stay with your parents for a year or two, you too could be in great financial position assuming you had no student loan debt and you invested properly.

2) *Asset Accumulation Stage*

The asset accumulation stage begins in your early twenties and goes on up until about age 50.

At this stage you would probably not have a lot of funds for investing, however you would have a high degree of debt relative to your net worth.

As you mature into your 30's and 40's your debt would decline, and your net worth would increase as you would then start investing more in your retirement accounts and other investments.

3) *Conservation/Protection Stage*

The conservation/protection stage begins when you have acquired some assets—usually in your late 30's or 40's and may last up until you retire or scale back on working full-time.

At this stage you would normally have an increase in cash flow, assets, and net worth—and a corresponding decrease in outstanding debt. At this point you would more than likely be concerned about maintaining all that you have acquired.

Your life expectancy, unemployment, disability, umbrella insurance and lack of an adequate retirement plan would now be more of a concern to you. If you did not properly establish a retirement savings plan during your formative years and/or your asset accumulation years, you would be particularly concerned at this stage.

4) *Distribution/Gifting Stage*

The distribution/gifting stage usually occurs after age 50, when you realize (particularly if you have started early with your financial planning) that you can afford to spend on things you never thought possible.

If you did your planning right or even partially right during your formative years, your asset accumulation years, and your conservation/protection years—you would possibly be in position to:

* purchase that car for your child

* pay for your grandchild's private school tuition

* take that expensive vacation that you always wanted

You could also possibly pursue any other desires that you always avoided due to finances and time constraints. Those desires would now possibly be attainable in this stage.

If you really did your planning right, you could still be acquiring assets (asset accumulation stage), conserving and protecting your assets (conservation/protection stage), and distributing gifts— during the distribution/gifting stage.

If you did your financial planning right this stage (distribution/gifting) <u>could actually begin in your forties and continue for the rest of your life.</u>

At this point (distribution/gifting stage) your finances would be in order, and you would want to enjoy the rest of your life as you would begin to really see the clock ticking at this stage.

At this stage you would feel that your finances were in balance, and you could see your money outlasting your life expectancy.

Closing Thoughts on Life Stages & Financial Planning

It is important to realize that it is not uncommon for you to be in different life stages at the same time but at varying degrees in each stage.

Always keep in mind that the best time for you to obtain <u>financial education</u> is "prior to" the time that you will actually have to make a decision!

By doing so, you put yourself and your family in control—which decreases the likelihood that you could be manipulated or otherwise dealt with unfairly.

In other words, you want to make the financial decision that is best for you and your family, not what's best for the salesperson or the company that they represent.

Now that you have a conceptual understanding of the Life Stages or Phases of Financial Planning—let's go to the **first chapter** and see why having a "Financially Alert Mind" is so important and then go to other chapters to see how you can increase your wealth in a comprehensive manner and improve your financial position in an intelligent, consistent, and proactive manner!

CHAPTER 1 Why You Must Have A "Financially Alert Mind"

Learn why you must be responsible for managing your credit and finances...

You must realize that it is better to have a "financially alert mind" than to be "sleep at the wheel" as you journey towards your financial freedom!

Part of <u>showing your love</u> to your family and yourself is having a **"Financially Alert Mind"**—meaning you must know how to respond appropriately to all that happens in your financial life.

By being financially alert you will be of the mindset that ***you must act*** *in a* ***proactive manner*** *as you move toward improving your credit and finances!*

It encompasses a higher level of thought and action than merely being financially literate!

Those who have **a financially alert mind** know how to invest in a manner that serves their best long-term interests and they cannot be led astray by scammers and others who do not have their best interest in mind.

There are many personal finance sites that can further help you gain a financially alert mind, and they include among others the following:

Note: All of the following are free sites or nominal rates—be sure to read the fine print and the terms of use.

Education

1) <u>www.realty-1-strategic-advisors.com</u>

provides you the opportunity to gain the comprehensive <u>preparation</u> and <u>knowledge</u> that you need to succeed financially.

It does so in an easy to understand and apply manner and is a great site for those who desire to build a strong foundation as they manage their credit, financial and real estate affairs. Unlike many sites, the mental aspect of credit and finance is looked at in a fresh and helpful manner

2) www.moneycrashers.com

provides an array of finance topics that you can benefit from and presents topics from a number of authors and sources

3) www.khanacademy.com

provides video and audio on saving, credit, budgeting and other financial topics and is a great site if you like learning in an audio or video style

4) UC Irvine Personal Financial Planning Course

provides personal finance course designed to educate you on personal finance and is a great course for those who like to learn in a course type format and includes over 20 lessons—many of which you can benefit from

5) TheWealthIncreaser.com

provides blog articles on timely financial topics that can help you and your family increase your net worth in an intelligent, consistent and proactive manner

Saving

1) www.Gosimplifi.com—helpful financial planning links that can help you save money and time

2) www.Mineeds.com—bidding on professional services

3) www.Wepay.com—collects secure payments

Spending

1) www.truaxis.com—bill shrinking

2) www.getpocketbook.com—bill managing

3) www.Viewpoints.com—strategic spending

Budgeting

1) www.mint.com provides budgeting tools and other tools for those who want to effectively manage their finances—one of the best free budgeting sites available

2) www.learnvest.com provides budgeting and other tools for those who want to manage their finances. Financial planning and other services offered for a stated fee

3)www.coupons.com great site for finding brand name coupon discounts

4) www.choosetosave.org helpful budgeting and saving site— particularly if you have excel on your computer (interactive budget)

5) www.thebudgetcalculator.com helpful budget or cash flow calculator

Investing

1) www.morningstar.com provides investment advice and research tools that are second to none

2) www.portfoliomonkey.com help in analyzing portfolios

3) www.esplannerbasic.com calculate retirement planning

4) www.kiplinger.com retirement planning calculator—and more

5) www.financialmentor.com free calculators for budgeting, mortgages and more—fee for various financial services

Real Estate

1) www.the-best-atlanta-real-estate-advice.com provides real estate advice and information that home buyers and home sellers need to know

2) www.zillow.com provides home buyer and home seller information in markets across the United States

3) www.trulia.com a close competitor to zillow—they too provide home buyer and home seller information in markets across the United States

4) www.realtytrac.com foreclosure tracking site that provides data on communities across the United States

5) www.city-data.com provides helpful demographic data on communities in the United States

6) www.Neighborhoodscout.com—make affordable home move—and demographic data of interest

7) www.greatschools.com provides school rankings in communities across the United States

8) www.financialmentor.com/mortgagecalculators provides mortgage calculators to help you plan your future—and more

9) www.realty-1-strategic-advisors.com provides finance, real estate, and other advice and information that home buyers and home sellers need to know

Other

www.Annualcreditreport.com—all-in-one site for tracking your credit and obtaining your free credit reports from all three major credit bureaus

www.MyFICO.com—get your credit score for a fee

www.CharityNavigator.com—making smart donations

www.Kayak.com—booking cheap flights

www.Mytab.com—trip saving site

www.HealthInReach.com—compare medical procedure costs

www.Socialpicks.com—share investment strategies

It is critical that you understand why having a financially alert mind is so important!

By gaining the knowledge that you need to succeed, you put yourself in position to take your credit and financial success higher—so that you can timelier achieve the goals that you and your family desire.

By making a real commitment to use your mind in a **financially alert manner** you can put yourself in position—to achieve your and your family's financial mission!

By opening your mind up to what is possible you put yourself in control of your credit and finances and your future!

A **"financially alert mind"** allows you to do your own thinking and allows **you** to **"take action"** on your own initiative so that you are empowered with the ability to achieve the goals that serve your and your family's best interest.

You won't have to be forced or inspired by others to act. You will act on your own initiative to create the future that you desire!

In a real sense that is what this book is all about—empowering you with the **working knowledge** that you need so that you can succeed!

Did you know that if you have the self-discipline, proper preparation, proper focus and the right knowledge that is necessary, you can manage many or all of the credit and financial affairs in your life?

Always realize that if you can control your thought process and direct your actions the right way, you can control your future now!

You can choose to "build up" your future or "tear down" your future by your daily thoughts and by the actions that you take on a consistent basis!

Did you know that a **F**inancially **A**lert **M**ind **I**mproves **L**ives **Y**early?

By having a **Financially Alert Mind** you can put yourself and your family in position to reach many or all of the future goals that you desire and you can attain the goals that can make a real difference in your and your family's life!

You can now show your **LOVE** to your family and benefit your **F A M I L Y** and yourself—by having a **Financially Alert Mind**—this year!

As a result of purchasing this book today, you can increase your and your family's net worth in a highly efficient and highly effective way!

It is imperative that you take responsibility for your future success as you must have the mindset that you (and only you) are responsible for your credit and financial future.

You take responsibility in a major way by planning for your future in a way that is most advantageous for you and your family.

It is important that you take "full responsibility" for your credit and financial future.

You must realize that it is "you" who must put in motion a plan that will take you and your family to where you need or want to be!

Do you know that many suffer financially due to irresponsible credit and money management and not lack of income?

In today's economy, you can't depend on others to improve your credit and finances for you.

You must always have a winning attitude and have an optimistic view of your credit and financial future.

Your attitude toward how you feel about yourself and your financial future will play a large part in helping you reach the goals and objectives that you desire for yourself and your family.

You must always realize that it is your responsibility to develop positive habits of success.

You must have a high level of determination to really make the goals that you seek a reality. It is your responsibility to develop and cultivate positive habits of success if your goal is to move yourself and your family forward in a meaningful way!

You must pursue sound physical health, have a positive mental attitude, have an energetic spirit, have the ability to control your thought process, have a big imagination (ability to dream big), and apply your faith daily!

You must show loyalty to others if you want loyalty, plan your future with others to reach a common goal, appreciate your life now by acting daily, have a purpose for living, have a pleasing personality and operate and take personal initiative on matters of importance during your time on earth!

There are things that you must condition your mind to always do if you desire to achieve more throughout life!

You must always budget your time, always be intelligent in thought (think carefully, analytically, accurately and critically), always give or do more than is expected, always cooperate with others in an effective manner, always respond favorably to adversity, always have self-discipline and self-confidence at all times and always have an enthusiastic spirit—if you "really" want to succeed at a high level.

You must always have thoughts of success on a consistent basis as by doing so you will defeat negative thoughts and negative behavior that does not serve your or your family's long term interest.

Although you can never really accomplish the above fully, you must have the aspirations to do so at a level that is the best that is within you!

You must transform or renew your mind from the inside out— and find new and more effective ways of thinking about matters of importance to you.

No one else can do it for you! It is your responsibility to formulate your mindset for a successful and prosperous future!

You have all that it takes on the inside to transform your mind and take your life in the direction that you desire. From this day forward you must not look for others to do it for you.

You can achieve great heights in your life if you have the desire to do so! You can cultivate habits of success to a high level and success will undoubtedly come if you have faith and "really" believe in your heart that you can do it.

In this book you have much of what you need to transform your credit and finances in a major way and build wealth efficiently!

However, it is your responsibility (totally within your "power" and "control") to bring a "high level" of determination, self-discipline, focus, personal initiative and other key qualities of success to the table, if you are "truly sincere" about improving your and your family's credit and finances to a high level.

You are responsible for knowing about and understanding personal financial statements that can really benefit you and your family, if used properly.

You are responsible for understanding how credit works and using that knowledge to manage and improve your and your family's credit and finance position.

You are responsible for knowing that "written goal setting" is far superior—to just thinking about your goals—and then trying to reach your goals!

Always remember, that even though you may be paying for financial advice and/or the financial management of your funds—it is still "your responsibility" to understand your risks and do your "due diligence" when choosing an advisor or planner in as effective a manner as possible!

You are responsible for understanding your personal finances in a comprehensive manner **and understanding the need for and "purpose" of a** properly funded emergency fund.

It Is your responsibility to act in a timely manner.

If you have the motivation on this day—positive credit and finance improvement is on the way!

You will set yourself apart—if you are now ready to start!

Real credit and finance solutions for you—are only pages away!

Will you make it a point to get serious—on this day?

You can no longer use "difficulty of understanding" as an excuse!

Get started now—and put The Wealth Increaser to good use!

Success lives in you—whether you believe it to be true!

It is important that you know (your responsibility) what is working in, for, though, around and against you regarding your credit and finances?

Do you know what is working in, for, though, around and against you in your credit and finances?

Are creditor's benefiting off of your unwise use of credit or do you have a pay-off or pay-down plan in place that will take you to where you need or desire to be?

Do you have an overall plan for success with your credit and finances (it is always best that you have an overall—or comprehensive approach to your credit and finances) or are you looking at your credit and finances in isolation?

Do you know your life purpose and the goals that you want to achieve in your life? Do you know the keys to success and the keys to avoiding failure?

Why You Must Take Responsibility

By "taking responsibility" you will put your mind in position to overcome whatever you are facing!

If you are now facing a difficult time whether it be financial or otherwise, you may feel that you have a lot of reasons to quit.

However, you must realize that if you decide to press on and move forward in spite of the adversity that you are now facing or that you may face in your future, you will be successful because you are already equipped (mental toughness) with what it takes to succeed.

However, if you don't believe that you are equipped (mental weakness)—you have already set yourself up for failure (you'll be a loser).

You must never underestimate the power of your thoughts on a daily basis!

Likewise, if you see success in your future—no matter how difficult your life may be or whatever comes your way, you set yourself up for the future success that you see and deserve!

Keep in mind that your journey may not be easy, but you must know that you will get there!

What You Must Do Now

You must realize that by "taking responsibility" for your future you can achieve much more than you anticipate and much more than you expect.

If you prepare your mind for future success by obtaining the knowledge that is necessary and you apply that knowledge effectively in your everyday life—your responsible use of your mind will be rewarded with success beyond your imagination!

At this point in time and space you must determine if you are a "do it now, direct action type of person" or are you one who will often procrastinate?

You must gear your mind up to get into the habit of doing what you need to do—NOW, if your goal is to achieve at a very high level!

By doing so you can achieve untold success in your credit and financial future from this day forward and build your wealth to a level that allows you to do what you desire during your lifetime.

You now have a real grasp of what you need to do (your responsibility) if you desire success at a high level, regardless of what stage you are at in your financial life!

Are you at this time disciplined enough to take responsibility for your and your family's future?

Now is the time for you to truly take responsibility for your future and achieve meaningful results!

Even though you may not have caused your current situation, it is your responsibility (how you got there is immaterial if you

decide to take responsibility now) to respond appropriately and in a manner that truly benefits you and your family.

Always realize that there is always a reason or excuse that you can give to explain your current situation and one that your mind will accept if "you" allow your mind to do so.

However, until you take responsibility for your current position and decide to take positive action to change your situation, you are operating in denial or fear!

By operating in denial or fear, you are showing that you are not ready to change, and you are not ready to take control of your finances—or any other area of your life where you are in denial!

By applying what you will learn throughout this book in a "sincere manner" you are showing that you are not only ready to change—you are demonstrating a real determination to change your future and that of your family's in a major way!

This book is for those who are "now ready" to change their future for the better in a major way and for those who have left excuses and blaming forces beyond their control for their current credit and finance position behind them!

The Wealth Increaser is not for those who are in denial about their credit and finances. Quite the contrary, this book is for those who know that they must take responsibility for their future and they know that they truly want to take on that responsibility in a manner that will take them to where they need or desire to be!

You can now utilize your mind in a responsible and meaningful way and in a way that can lead to you addressing your credit and finances in a comprehensive manner as you build wealth.

You can achieve more because unlike those who are financially literate, you are putting yourself in position to not only attain financially literacy, but you are putting yourself in position to attain a financially alert mind that will allow you to achieve more throughout your lifetime.

By doing so you reduce the stress in your and your family's life and you will make your and your family's years on planet earth—a more pleasurable experience!

You will also rightfully take the responsibility that you were enshrined with at birth to improve your and your family's net worth!

Now that you have a "comprehensive overview" of what you need to do on a consistent basis, let's go to the heart of this book and see what you can do in an intelligent manner to enhance your and your family's future for the better, and gain the needed insight to manage and increase your and your family's net worth!

CHAPTER 2 Why A Properly Established Emergency Fund Is a Requirement if You Desire Major Success

Emergency Funds Are Crucial in Today's Economy

<u>Why You Need An Emergency Fund:</u>

You achieve more when you set goals—limitless and largely untapped areas of accomplishment can occur—if you remove limitations from your mind and you set meaningful goals!

It is important that you live intentionally and with purpose—you dream big, and you plan and create your future in advance.

You must lead your life as well as manage your life! You must realize that setting goals provide you the direction that you need to go in a more precise manner, so that you can truly reach your goal(s)—and further helps you achieve what you desire most for you and your family in a timelier manner.

You can activate your brain to do more if you are aware of what you desire (your focus will be magnified) and when your big dream is brought to your mental awareness, you can do more!

You must make **properly establishing an emergency fund** one of your primary goals that you must achieve so that you can move your family forward currently and at the various stages of your life!

It is important that you realize that the primary purpose of an emergency fund is to carry you and your family through difficult financial times in a manner where you would not have to tap into other sources of income or your personal assets at the time of an unplanned emergency.

An emergency fund would provide funds so that you and your family would not have to use credit, retirement funds, borrowing and/or investment funds or other means—if you and your family were faced with a sudden and unexpected event.

Unexpected emergencies (job loss, major appliance repair or replacement, heating and air repair or replacement, automobile repairs etcetera) seem to happen all too frequently when you don't have an emergency fund—less so when you have a properly established emergency fund.

Emergency funds are meant to be there when you need them and should be invested in money market or other low risk accounts such as savings, CD's etcetera.

With the return on savings rate so low now, many are looking for higher returns by going online to find savings accounts that offer a higher yield. Be sure you are aware of the restrictions and make sure you thoroughly understand the fine print if you are searching for a higher rate of return.

You can go to bankrate.com to make sure that the banking institution earns at least 3 stars for safety.

You can go to moneyrates.com and other financial sites to find banks that offer higher yields than you are currently getting.

DepositAccounts.com offers you a daily update of savings and money market rates from a number of banks in the United States.

Also, consider longer term CD's that offer higher interest rates but have low penalty fees for early withdrawal. Again, be aware of the fine print and pay special attention to penalties. If you are forced to withdraw early you want an account that will still give you a good effective yield, therefore be sure to find a company that has low penalties or fees for early withdrawal.

You can go to bankrate.com/cd to learn more about banking institutions that offer low penalty CD's.

Use Caution if You Are Considering I Bonds in Your Emergency Fund Portfolio

Although not often looked at by many, an **I Bond** is another relatively safe option. An I Bond is a bond issued by the U.S. government and is reset twice a year to keep up with inflation. As of 08/2011 the rate was 4.6% on an annualized basis, however there is a five-year holding period and a $10,000 annual investment limit. If you pull your money out early there would be a penalty.

Let's say you pull your money out after 12 months—you would still earn over 2% which is still higher than what most banks are paying now (average of less than 1% at most banks as of 08/2011). If you purchase an I Bond, and the new rate goes up at the time of future resets you could earn even more.

As of 08/2023 the rate was 4.3% for bonds issued from May 2023 to October 2023.

You can buy I Bonds and check your returns directly at treasurydirect.gov and learn more about I Bonds by going to that site. Keep in mind that you can't redeem an I-Bond for one year. A staggered purchase approach or utilizing a portion of your emergency fund balance would generally be a more reasonable approach than using your total emergency fund for the purchase of I Bonds.

If you were to seriously consider I Bonds you must factor in the holding period as "emergencies" do not respect the one year holding period—or any holding period.

Bond Funds

On some occasions I have worked with clients who used conservative bond funds in their emergency fund.

A fund with an attractive yield (say—4% to 10%), low risk, and sound investment strategies (such as government backed securities, medium-term U.S., and corporate bonds at the right mix) and experienced management may appear to be a safe place to park emergency fund money—however, when interest rates rise the bond price will fall.

If you were to actively monitor your future risks by staying aware of market data, such as interest rate movement (upward movement of the ten-year treasury yield) you could come out ahead if you moved the money in a timely manner to safer areas such as a money market account.

However, for most emergency funds—a bond fund is still not the ideal place to park money for a true emergency, even though the risk of loss may not appear that great on the surface.

Why Many Have Difficulty Establishing an Emergency Fund

Emergency Funds are often difficult to establish for many due to inadequate income (all income is needed for daily living), lack of focus, lack of awareness and with many—they just plainly don't want an emergency fund as they feel all their income outside of daily living should be invested in assets that provide a better return than that of a money market account or CD.

This can often be the wrong approach as the account could lose substantial value. However, many use this approach due to not properly understanding the "purpose" of an emergency fund.

Again, be sure to utilize low risk savings vehicles for your emergency fund!

It is also important to establish an emergency fund at the earliest time possible. The earlier in your "financial life phase" that you establish an emergency fund, the more effective you can be at attaining your other financial goals and objectives.

Establishing an emergency fund at the earliest time possible is an important step in "improving your financial position" and that of your family's.

Aim for a 6-month emergency fund (6 months of salary—or 6 months of living expenses) at a minimum and build on that even more if you see the need to do so.

By establishing this fund early in your financial life, you will put yourself and your family in a winning financial position where you have a solid foundation to build upon.

Also, be sure to avoid unnecessary fees:

Be sure not to tap into your emergency fund unless there is a true emergency and be sure to avoid monthly or recurring fees for inactive accounts.

To avoid inactivity and other fees you may have to set up monthly deposits of a certain amount, utilize a number of debit purchases or utilize other creative ways to avoid inactivity fees. You must be aware of all the fees involved at your institution and you must find a way to reduce or eliminate those fees if they negatively affect your emergency fund balance.

Debt Payoff or Debt Reduction Is Critical for Your Success

Closely related to establishing your emergency fund is to keep your credit card balances low and pay off your balance monthly. You don't want to be in a position where you are paying credit card debt at 15% or more and you have a 6-month emergency fund where you are earning 1% to 5%.

Be sure you are in position to pay off your credit card balance monthly after or while your emergency fund is established. Doing so will not only maintain and improve your credit score, but will provide you with a properly funded emergency fund that can be used for true emergencies.

You put yourself in position to pay off your debt by establishing a personal budget or cash flow statement at a minimum!

You will also want to establish a **personal income statement** and a **personal balance sheet** so that you can see where you now stand as far as your **net worth** is concerned.

To manage your credit and future debt more effectively you want to have **mastery of the five credit factors** so that you manage your credit to your advantage throughout your lifetime or during the period that you desire to or are forced to use credit.

In the **next six chapters** we will address what you need to do in an **intelligent, consistent, and proactive basis** in the area of **insurance, investments, taxes, education planning, estate planning/wills and retirement planning** to achieve lasting success.

In the **final chapter** we will further reiterate the effort that will be required by you—if you are truly sincere in making your dreams come true. You will learn how to pull together the **"3 Step Structured Approach"** so that you can manage your finances and build wealth with less effort!

CHAPTER 3 Insurance & What You Need to Know

Learn if you know all your insurance needs...

To obtain competitive insurance rates you can go to www.aigdirect.com and www.ehealthinsurance.com and www.policygenius.com.

Insurance Basics

Below we will discuss basic levels of insurance that you should not only be familiar with but should be a part of your mental framework when you are evaluating insurance products— whether for yourself and/or your family.

You must know all of the insurance products that can be of benefit to you and your family and you must realize that it is your responsibility to put in place a plan that reflects that responsible use of your mind.

You must evaluate the need for and actual selection of the appropriate insurance products—that are discussed below.

Automobile

Key concerns are your liability limits, and you want to at least have the **standard 100/300/100 coverage** which means you have $100,000 coverage per person for bodily injury, including death that you cause to others, $300,000 in bodily injury per accident and property damage up to $100,000. If you have a high net worth—consider increasing the amount even higher.

You can do so by purchasing a **personal umbrella policy** that increases your liability limits even higher.

Used in conjunction with your home or renter's policies you can get coverage of a million dollars or more for $300 or so on an annual basis—possibly more.

Add several hundred more dollars and you can easily increase the amount to 3 or 4 million—which would provide you added comfort, particularly if you have a high net worth or high income.

It is also important that you know your **medical payments or personal injury protection coverage** on your policy.

The required coverage varies by state, but if you had the coverage, you would be protected if you had an accident and you had relatively small medical expenses for yourself and others who were injured in an accident, regardless of who was at fault!

Personal injury protection would normally cover lost wages, loss of services, and funeral expenses.

If you have a late model vehicle or one that is valued at a high level—consider **collision /comprehensive coverage** that can cover damage to your car that is not covered by the policy of the driver that collided with your vehicle.

Comprehensive provides coverage for fire, flood, falling trees, hail, hurricane, or animal strikes in many states.

Be sure you have a properly funded emergency fund if you have a high deductible policy.

Even though you may lower your payments with a higher deductible policy—you still must have cash on hand to pay the deductible effectively—and in as stress-free a manner as possible.

In today's economy be sure to get uninsured/under-insured motorist coverage at the level of your standard policy at a minimum—and increase that amount if you are a high earner or have a high net worth.

You will be protected in the event of a hit and run or if someone hits you and they do not have appropriate insurance coverage. In many states it is not uncommon for 20% or more of the drivers on the road to be under-insured or driving without any insurance at all!

You must also realize that your credit score will play a role in the monthly premium that you will pay in virtually all states except California. Many insurers have concluded that those drivers with lower credit scores get into more accidents.

In addition, your driving record (affects your insurance rate for life, health and auto) and your vehicles horsepower is a critical factor in determining your insurance premium.

Debt Elimination

In today's economy it is essential that you eliminate or reduce your debt in as effective a manner as possible and you properly establish an emergency fund.

By doing "both" you are taking real action to "ensure" a prosperous and productive future for yourself and your family.

After paying off or paying down your debt—be sure not to repeat the debt cycle. Be sure to pay your credit purchases off in a timely manner (i.e., monthly) if possible, and at a minimum try to keep your overall credit utilization under 10%.

By doing so consistently, you are protecting your future and preserving a way of life that you can pass on to your future generations.

Disability Insurance

Another key area of concern that you must address if you are in position to do so is disability insurance. It can protect you from an unforeseen disability that could lead to severe losses of income while you are recovering from covered disabilities.

Emergency Fund

Although not insurance in the purest sense—properly establishing and maintaining an <u>emergency fund</u> will provide you and your family with the protection that you need to help you avoid life's inevitable risks that will come your way.

Although it takes <u>focus</u>, <u>effort</u>, <u>determination</u> and <u>planning</u> to properly establish an emergency fund, it is something that you "must" do if you desire success at a high level when choosing your insurance products along with building wealth efficiently.

Be sure to properly reduce or eliminate your debt prior to, or while you are establishing your emergency fund. By doing so you can put yourself and your family in real position—for real success!

Group Health Insurance

You can often get insurance at a lower rate and with broader coverage if you participate in group health plans whether on the job or provided in other group settings.

Group Life Insurance

You can also often get group life insurance at a lower rate if you participate in group life plans whether on the job or provided in other group settings.

Health Insurance

Health insurance is an area that you must address as rising health costs and your inability to pay for medical procedures and preventive **health care** measures out of pocket are rising far faster than the cost of inflation.

Homeowners Insurance

Insuring your home is a requirement if you currently have a mortgage on your home—and is optional if you own your home free and clear!

It is imperative that you know what is covered, you know your coverage limits and you know the riders that you not only have in place—but the riders that you need.

Riders protect you and provide additional coverage for things that are not covered in the standard policy.

Common riders include:

- Jewelry

- Flood Insurance

- Art

- Many Others

Also be aware of percentage deductibles and what they cover—and know what is excluded if you are in a state that offers them, and they are a part of your policy.

The standard policy covers damage caused by major threats—to a limit—such as fire, hail, wind, lightning, falling trees, tornadoes, cars, and vandals, among others.

Earthquakes, hurricanes and flooding by rivers or levees are not covered under the standard policy. Therefore, you would have to purchase additional coverage.

Your furniture, electronics, clothing, tools, and other personal belongings would be covered.

The standard policy also provides you coverage for liability if someone was injured on your property or if you or other family members—including your dog—caused damage to others.

Liability coverage is normally $100,000; however, you can increase that amount if you choose too, and in today's "lawsuit" society you want to have at least $300,000.

Be sure to consider raising your deductibles to help reduce your premiums and be sure you have a properly funded emergency fund in place, or you are working toward that goal.

Also be sure that you are aware of personal umbrella policies, and you know how they can benefit you and your family.

Standard Homeowner policies often called **HO 2 or HO 3 policies** normally cover damage to your home or other structures on your lot—such as garages, storage sheds, fencing—etcetera.

Be sure to insure your home at "replacement value" as that amount is in almost all cases higher than your appraised value, market value—or tax assessed value.

It is also wise to select the "extended coverage rider" that can protect you from rising building costs after a natural disaster. By selecting that rider, you can get up to an additional 30% of coverage on top of the replacement cost that it could take to rebuild your home.

In addition, it is wise to purchase an "ordinance" or "law endorsement rider" which pays the higher cost of making repairs that conform to current building codes.

If you are purchasing a home in the future, be sure that you are aware of the history of the home as far as insurance claims and you have properly addressed <u>environmental concerns</u>—that you may have with the home—and the surrounding community—that you are considering moving into!

Home Business Insurance

If you have a home business, you must realize that the contents of your business may not be insured under your standard home or renter's policy—or may be covered only to a stated limit.

Depending on your business you may need to increase your liability levels, insure your equipment and inventory—and seriously analyze the need for added coverage in other areas.

*Keep in mind that in most states an endorsement does not cover liability related to your business—**therefore, you would need "a small business insurance package"** which would protect your business property at home, or on the road and cover liability for theft and loss of income to a limit.*

In many states it is inexpensive (several hundred dollars a year)—so you should purchase a policy if you want additional protection in a cost-effective manner.

Be sure to get a quote from your current insurer first and if you feel they are too high search the insurance marketplace to find a better rate.

Be sure to select a highly rated company and be sure to do your due diligence on the front end—not after the policy is selected!

Life Insurance

Life insurance is critical for your and your family's future and you should obtain the right amount at a highly rated company.
Did you know that there are a number of ways that you can determine your and your family's insurance needs?

Obtaining life insurance is a critical component of transferring wealth and you should be in the game at some level—regardless of your income if you have dependents and you want to position them for success after your unfortunate transition.

Long-Term Care

Long-term care is an area of insurance that is fairly new in popularity (last 25 years or so) but should be of real concern to you as you approach age 50 and beyond.

Does it appear that you qualify for Medicare?

Are you on track to reach your financial and retirement goals and do you know if you will have a need for (Long-Term Care) LTC insurance?

Are you in position to self-insure or have you purchased LTC insurance—or do you have a plan in place to purchase LTC insurance based on current premiums—and the way that LTC insurance now operates?

These are questions that you must ask yourself and answer appropriately if you want to address your long-term care needs appropriately.

Renters Insurance

Rental insurance will protect your contents that you may have inside a property that you are currently renting. Owners of rental properties will normally have insurance on the structure—however the **insuring of the contents that are inside** is your responsibility!

Be sure to obtain the coverage that you need at a highly rated company.

Standard rental insurance is often called **HO 4** and it would protect the loss of your personal property from fire, theft, and other specified losses and they too include liability coverage so you can increase those limits as well.

If you have auto insurance as well, you can purchase an umbrella insurance policy that provides additional liability protection for you and your family.

If you don't have an auto, you can still increase the liability levels on your rental policy.

Also keep in mind that the standard renter's policy does not cover losses from floods, earthquakes, sewer backups, hurricanes (where available) and other perils—therefore, you must purchase an additional policy or add endorsements or riders to your existing renter's policy.

Personal Liability (Umbrella Insurance Coverage)

Another area of insurance that you need is personal liability and be sure to get it at the appropriate level.

If you have a high net worth be sure to seriously consider your need for and potential benefit of this protection.

If you have auto, home or rental insurance and you have a high net worth or you are a high-income earner, the purchase of additional levels of personal liability coverage should be given real consideration.

For just a few hundred dollars annually you can gain coverage of one million dollars or more with many highly rated insurance companies.

Personal Liability or an Umbrella Insurance Policy would protect you and your family in a similar manner that an umbrella would protect you from the elements.

You would not get as wet— (lose as much financially if you were faced with a liability issue of a high amount)—if you increased your liability levels on your and your family's policy.

By purchasing an umbrella policy (particularly if you are a high earner or have a high net worth) you can further protect your home, investment assets, vehicles, and other valuables that you may possess.

Again, a Personal Umbrella Liability policy increases your liability protection to a higher level than that which is stated in your standard policy on your auto, home or renter's policy!

It is a cost-effective way to increase your liability coverage and should be given strong consideration.

CHAPTER 4 Investments & What You Need to Know

Learn why you must have a basic understanding of investments...

Over the years we have seen many consumers invest in there and their family's financial future. Many have done quite well over the years despite investing in a haphazard manner.

Many others have invested in a haphazard (inappropriate) manner and did not reach their desired goals.

Still others have invested in a manner that worked for them in <u>good and bad times</u>—by investing properly.

In this chapter our goal is to explain investing in a manner that will maximize your opportunity to attain the investment goals that you desire while you put an investment plan in place.

You already know that you need to reduce or eliminate your debt. By going to **Appendix A**, you can find a blueprint of how to achieve the debt payoff or debt pay down goals that you desire and plan for a successful retirement!

If you are **<u>determined and serious</u>** and you have made up in "your heart and mind" that you are willing to **<u>"put into action"</u>** a plan and work toward achieving the success that you desire—you now have a blueprint that allows you to do so at your fingertips!

By properly analyzing **Appendix A** and utilizing the knowledge that you will learn throughout this book, you will gain the **<u>preparation</u>** and **<u>knowledge</u>** that will lead to true and lasting success for yourself and your family if that is what you desire!

You can no longer use "cost" or "difficulty of understanding" as an excuse to not reduce or eliminate your debt or improve your finances.

You can now put your mind and heart to good use. Starting today, you can utilize your mind in a more effective way!

You must "put into action" all that you are learning if you desire success at a high level!

Just thinking or believing you can do it or depending on others is not enough! If you have true faith in your financial (and life) future, you will put into action that which you know can truly benefit you and your family.

By doing so you will achieve the success that you desire because there can be no other outcome.

If you are truly operating in faith and you have the right preparation and the right knowledge operating inside of your mind—there can be no other outcome other than the success that you desire!

Always remember that faith is taking action—not inaction or reaction!

Did you know that if you change your thoughts you can change your future and create the future that you desire, not the future that others desire that you have?

You must have a basic understanding of what you need to know to maximize your chance for investment success and you must apply that understanding and knowledge in a manner that works best for your and your family's long-term success.

You can achieve success in your investments if you approach the process from the right angle.

You must arm yourself with the knowledge that you need and apply that knowledge if you are to attain success on a consistent basis and in a manner that is in your and your family's best interest.

OK—you say, all that sound great, but what do I need to do to invest properly in good and bad times right now?

You must realize that if you have the **self-discipline** and **mental focus** that is needed (or you are willing to cultivate those qualities to a higher level) and **you are willing to take direct action on a consistent basis** you can invest successfully by comprehending and applying what you will learn in the following paragraphs!

Eliminate or Reduce Your Debt

You must realize that if you started your investing prior to **reducing or eliminating your debt**, you are making future success for yourself and your family much more difficult to attain.

By reducing or eliminating your debt in an effective manner you are taking a "giant step" towards reaching your and your family's future goals and objectives.

Establish an Emergency Fund

The establishment of a properly funded emergency fund along with the reduction and/or elimination of your debt lies at the center of your future success. You must have a **"safe place"** to park your cash for life's unexpected happenings!

A job loss, a car breakdown, major plumbing repairs and the like seem to happen all too frequently when you don't have an emergency fund, less so when you have one!

Be sure to use **"personal financial statements"** to assist you in your debt reduction or debt payoff goals—as well as your emergency fund goals!

Address Your Insurance Needs

You must look at your insurance needs from **all angles** and come up with a plan to purchase the coverage that you need in all areas.

By properly obtaining the **coverage that is needed** you put in motion the protection that is needed to move forward in a manner that serves you and your family more effectively.

Address Your Tax Position

Do you know your current tax position? Do you even care to know?

Although you don't have to be a tax expert on tax matters, there are certain areas of taxation that you must understand and know how to effectively utilize.

You must look at your taxes as far as property, personal income, capital gains and other areas of taxation that affect you and your family and then improve your tax position as best you can, based on your current life stage.

Address Your Education Planning

Are you contemplating higher education in the future for yourself or your children? If you are, you must know the steps that you need to take to do the necessary planning in an efficient manner!

Due to the "time horizon" that may be involved you want to be in position to start the process as early as possible.

By doing so you can obtain the needed "education" that you need and use the "time value of money" to your benefit to reach your (or your family members) education planning goals.

Address Your Estate Planning/Wills

Have you contemplated your family's future if you were to transition in an **untimely manner?**

As difficult as it may be to confront it is still something that you "must do."

By doing so, you put your family in a better position for success— if you were to transition unexpectedly!

Address Your Retirement

Retirement Planning is critical for you and your family regardless of where you are at in your **life stage**!

Do you have a plan in place that provides you the **opportunity** to live at the level that you now live at (or a higher level)?

You must have a **highly effective retirement plan** in place that provides you the ability to live at the level that you desire!

After properly analyzing and addressing the above in an appropriate manner you are now ready to invest in a highly effective manner!

Now that you have analyzed and improved upon all the major areas of your finances and addressed them effectively and in a comprehensive manner, you are now ready to invest in a manner that serves your and your family's best interest!

You now know that understanding the "basics of investing" starts well before you begin to invest.

You now know that you can choose to invest on a whim, and you might reach the goals that you desire—however, you know that it is not the best approach to take!

You can use your mind to choose to invest in a wise manner or an unwise manner! You now have access to **powerful information** on the way to invest properly.

The **choice** that you make will determine your and your family's future outcomes as it relates to your finances in a major way!

You can choose to invest in a haphazard manner and possibly have a successful future or you can choose to invest in "a more appropriate manner" and truly position yourself and your family for the future success that you desire on a consistent and highly effective basis!

You now know that if you address all of the major areas of your finances and "then" start your investment journey—you increase your likelihood for success and you increase your likelihood of reaching the investment goals that serve your and your family's best interest!

Most importantly, you now know that you should not be swayed by those who urge you to invest on a whim, whether it be your favorite radio personality, entertainer, professional athlete, con-artist or anyone else, if your goal is to invest properly and in a manner that truly serves the best interest of you and your family!

You now or soon will know that you can properly address all of the areas of your finances listed above by mentally comprehending and applying what you are now learning in this book at a level that is the best that is within YOU!

By doing so you have the potential to attain major success **in your and your family's future!**

Investments & Purchasing YOUR PERSONAL RESIDENCE

Due to the importance of buying a home and wealth building, purchasing a home will be discussed in a manner where if you do it properly—it can not only be an investment, but it can help you build your wealth in a relatively painless way as you have to live somewhere anyway.

Purchasing and selling your home the right way and investments are closely related.

If you purchase and/or sell your home appropriately, you will have money left over so that you can invest outside of your retirement accounts.

It is important that prior to purchasing your home or soon afterward, you establish a **six month emergency fund** or you have other "compensating factors" at work that will put you in a strong financial position prior to purchasing your personal residence, or soon afterward.

Be sure that you are fully covered **INSURANCE wise**—that means life, home, auto, umbrella liability, health, disability and long-term care have all been addressed at or before the time of your home purchase.

Your INVESTMENTS outside of **RETIREMENT** prior to purchasing your home may not be critical at the time of purchase—however, you should have a solid amount of **discretionary income** left over after the purchase of your home.

However, it is critical that you know your **TAX situation** and improve upon it prior to purchasing your home—if at all possible.

That means that you should be taking home most of your potential tax refund monthly by adjusting your withholding.

By doing so you would get a smaller refund (that will also protect you against tax fraud where someone uses your information and gets the refund that was owed to you—and therefore delays your tax refund) on your state and federal income taxes—if that applies to you.

If you have children, and/or you anticipate having **EDUCATIONAL expenses** in the future—whether for yourself, your spouse or your children—it is important that you take a look at saving for the expenses. However, it may not be critical that you have a plan in place prior to purchasing your home.

It would really depend on the time horizon and the expected cost of the educational expenses in the future as well as in-state versus out-of-state tuition and a host of other specific factors unique to your situation.

Let's assume that you are currently age 29 and your spouse is age 27—and you have two kids aged 5 and 7—and you are saving 20% annually with a 5% match on your 401k.

Your spouse is also saving $5,000 per year in ROTH IRA'S to further fund your retirement and you currently have a balance of $110,000 in total in all your retirement accounts.

As for your **ESTATE PLANNING & WILLS** you should analyze and update them on an annual basis generally—as life changes can have a positive or negative effect on your ESTATE PLANNING & WILLS.

If your NET WORTH or INCOME is not at a high level you may not need ESTATE PLANNING at this time! However, you and your spouse should still have a separate WILL that spells out your intentions and wishes should one or both of you transition unexpectedly.

By analyzing at some level your financial needs in the area of your **i**nsurance, **i**nvestments, **t**axes, **e**mergency fund, **e**ducation planning, **e**state planning/wills and **r**etirement planning you put yourself and your family in better position for long-term wealth building success.

Investor Success Tips

At this time, we are making the assumption that you have properly" assessed your financial situation" and you have a six-to-twelve-month emergency fund, you are adequately insured, your tax situation is at a level that benefits you the most, you have an educational savings plan in place or anticipate starting one, and you and your spouse have updated your will.

You are now ready to invest outside of your RETIREMENT accounts. You save 20% annually with a 5% match on your 401k (maximum contribution allowed for 2023 is $22,500) and $5.000 per year on a ROTH IRA for your spouse.

You are currently renting a home at $1,500 per month. You and your spouse have saved $60,000 for the down payment on your home and still have a 12-month emergency fund ($24,000)— based on your current monthly bills.

Your income is $80,000 per year and your spouse's income is $40,000. You have no outstanding credit card or revolving debt, nor do you have any outstanding car loans or installment debt.

At this time, you are now "Ready, Willing and Able" to Invest

We will now look at the more common investment vehicles that are available to you when investing outside of your retirement accounts.

- Savings: CD's, Money Market Mutual Funds & Money Market Accounts
- Checking Accounts: Various Types—Debit Card usually tied to this Account
- Bonds: Tax—Tax Free—Corporate—Municipal
- Stocks: Various Sectors
- Mutual Funds: Various Sectors
- Exchange Traded Funds: Various Sectors
- REIT'S or **Real Estate Investment Trusts**
- Real Estate
- Other: Art, Collectibles, Commodities, Precious Metals, Crypto Currency, FOREX etcetera

You decide that your first investment outside of retirement and excluding the emergency fund will be in the form of a home for you and your family.

Because you have everything in place to make your home purchase enjoyable, you should be in a great position for home ownership!

Many financial planners do not see your personal home as an investment, however if you do it right—it can be an investment.

By purchasing a property where you can live at—or preferably—below your means—you will have MORE money left over to invest outside of retirement or invest MORE toward your retirement.

Therefore, it is important that you realize that properly purchasing your home is an investment in you, your future and your family's future and you can successfully use the purchase of your home to build wealth efficiently if you approach your home purchase with the right mindset.

In addition, the potential is there for the property to appreciate at a level higher than that of inflation and at the time you decide to sell—you could possibly see a large "tax free" gain—if you make the proper purchase and subsequent sell within certain parameters.

Furthermore, you must live somewhere anyway!

The key is to purchase in a neighborhood that you are comfortable in and has strong schools, strong government management, strong infrastructure and purchase at a price that will leave you with high discretionary income and gives you the best chance to enjoy life and save "in and outside of" your retirement accounts.

Once you have the retirement projections that you and your spouse feel are adequate for your retirement years, you would then be ready to invest outside of your retirement accounts.

By having your future retirement accounts in place and targeted amounts (retirement number) that you will need in the future relatively certain, investing outside of your retirement accounts (whether it be real estate or any of the financial vehicles listed above) will be less stressful—in fact, you should feel comfortable and good about doing it!

By being in such strong financial investing position your mindset(s) should be:

If we lost everything "outside of our retirement accounts and emergency fund" we would still have a great life and our retirement years would be enjoyable. And our kids educational and other expenses—"still" would be taken care of.

In addition, you would be enjoying life along the way as you can meet all your living expenses quite easily and you have discretionary income available that allows you to live at a level that is comfortable for you and your family—and in line with the lifestyle that you desire.

The theory behind this type of strategy is that you should be able to lose all that you invest outside of your retirement and emergency fund and still be set financially— (reach your target) in your retirement years and have your and your families future educational and other goals met on a consistent basis.

If you like to purchase a car every several years or so, these expenses should also be met with your discretionary income that you have on a monthly or annual basis.

In actual practice we know that the odds that you would lose all that you invest outside of retirement would be very low (unless you were to choose highly speculative investment vehicles)— however if you did you would still be in a great position, because you have your financial house "in order."

If you decide to invest conservatively outside of retirement with money market accounts or CD's, that would be appropriate if that is what you were comfortable with.

As long as the amounts invested outside of retirement does not affect your monthly living conditions or emergency fund—it would be appropriate for you to invest a certain amount each month outside of retirement.

If you are conservative in your investment philosophy, you could also choose to invest in riskier or more exotic type investments— if you chose to do so.

By having your financial house "in order" you would be in position to do that, and a loss would not "materially" affect your living conditions and that of your family's, either now or during your retirement years.

Other Key Investment Points:

In the above illustration the couple makes $120,000 annually with 25% ($30,000) going towards taxes and health insurance—and 20% ($24,000) going towards their retirement.

Assuming they both worked until age 60—they would have over 30 years of investment earnings within their retirement accounts (retirement contributions alone would be over a million dollars— and with earnings they could have a "nest egg" of several million dollars to enjoy during their retirement years).

They have $66,000 left over (after payment of taxes, health insurance and retirement contributions) to live off in a 12-month period or $5,500 per month.

By purchasing a home with a total monthly payment of $1,500 (just over 27% of their monthly income)—after taxes, health insurance and retirement contributions, they would be in a "winning lifetime position" by purchasing a home well below their means.

They have $5,500 left over monthly for their mortgage, electric, gas, food, maintenance, and other common monthly expenses. Assuming their monthly expenses total $3,500, that would leave them with $2,000 in discretionary income that they could spend— or save (INVEST)—any way that they liked.

The above situation is a great position for them to be in. They are in position to do several positive financial maneuvers.

They could accumulate rapid savings rather quickly to increase their emergency fund, invest risky if they so choose to do so, take the kinds of vacations that they want to take and not be limited in their choices due to finances, purchase an investment property— or reach many other goals that they may have for their family.

What It All Means

The point of this chapter is that the home purchaser's and investors are in total control of their financial lives. They are not floating along being pulled in different directions by "MURPHY" because they have a comprehensive view of their finances and financial future.

They know that they have a bright and prosperous future, and it will show in their daily behavior and the way they approach life. They have an inner peace within and it is largely due to the "choices" that they made.

They know that by using "written goal setting" they see their future in clear terms and their focus is magnified and their dreams are actually "brought to life."

Contrast the above scenario of a family in the same scenario—but they purchase a property with a payment of $3,000 per month and they are carrying revolving and installment debt.

Although on the surface it may appear that they are doing exceedingly well, life could possibly be miserable for them.

Basically, properly purchasing a home and investing properly IS highly correlated and the success or failure in your financial life could depend on the choices that you make prior to, while and after your home purchase.

This cannot be "overstated"—as many who try to enjoy life by putting the horse before the cart (making financial decisions in the wrong order) fall victim to unfortunate financial conditions that could have easily been avoided had they made the proper choice at the proper time and not over-extending on their spending.

What You Can Do Now

Whether you and your spouse earn six figures or just enough to get by on—you can start on a path to achieve the success that you desire. Just as the couple above did, so too can you. You must start where you are at and not procrastinate!

If you earn $40,000 per year and your spouse earns $20,000 per year—just apply the same general concepts and you will be on your way to success at a higher level of certainty.

Likewise, if you earn even more—say $160,000 per year and your spouse earns $80,000 per year, you will again apply the same general concepts and you will be on your way to success—and at a higher level of certainty.

Why Action Is All That Really Matters

If you apply what you have just learned at your highest level and in a sincere manner—you will have no reason or excuse for not reaching your and your family's future goals.

You must act today, by doing so a brighter future can be on the way!

You no longer have an excuse—if you now put your mind to good use!

By acting now—and properly applying what you are learning—you will soon say wow!

It is imperative that you have the <u>mental working knowledge</u> to make <u>good decisions</u> and <u>good choices</u> when it comes to your credit and finances. By <u>properly applying what you are learning at this time</u> you are putting yourself in position to do just that!

CHAPTER 5 Taxes & What You Need to Know

Learn about tax basics and what you must know about taxes...

Tax planning is a broad area; however you want to at a minimum be aware of the basics so that you will have some idea of what you may need to act on when you meet with and communicate with your tax professional or with the managing of your financial affairs in general.

Business Taxation

If you are a business owner, be sure to choose the business structure that is the best choice from a liability and tax point of view for the type of business that you have, and your current and long-term goals.

Be sure you know what a **w-9 form** is—and know how it affects you and your business.

Be sure you are aware of the tax laws (or hire competent professionals) that affect your business, and tax plan far in advance, not after damage has occurred or in the middle of a transaction.

If you have a home-based business, you can now deduct your home office expense in a less burdensome manner—since the passage of new regulations in 2012.

Capital Gains

If you have capital gains during the year you can offset those gains (up to $3,000) against losses. If more than$3,000 in losses, you carry the losses forward for use in future years.

In 2013 the capital gain rate for many taxpayers, depending on income increased from 15% to 20%.

If you have taxable income of $400,000 (individual) and $450,000 (joint return) any amount over that amount would be taxed at 20%. Also realize that there is a net investment income tax of 3.8% on modified adjusted gross income over certain thresholds.

Debt Cancellation

It is important that you realize that the **cancellation and reduction of "certain debt"** may be taxable to you. It is your responsibility to know this on the front end, prior to engaging in a debt settlement or debt reduction with any of your creditors!

In addition, if you fail to pay certain debt—creditors can go after you for the shortfall in many cases, if they decide to do so!

Estate Taxes

With the January 2023 update of taxes—estate taxes receive some clarification as the first $12.92 million in individual estates— and $25.84 million for family estates are now exempted from the estate tax.

After that the rate will be 40%, up from 35%—and the exemption amounts are now indexed for inflation.

Lifetime gifts that do not qualify for the **annual exclusion** will reduce the amount of gift and estate tax exemption available at death.

Excise & Other Taxes

Excise and other taxes that go by various names are also here to stay. Whether they called them fees, licensing—or the like, expect for them to increase in the future as utilities, local, state, and federal revenue must be created to fund the operations of government.

Health Savings Accounts

What they are:

An account (similar to a **flexible spending account**) that is often used to pay medical expenses that occur for an individual or family that has **major tax advantages** that include the following:

- *Contributions that are tax deductible* **(or contributions that are made on a pre-tax basis—if made through your employer's plan)**
- *Contributions and earnings that grow tax deferred*
- *Contributions and earnings that can be used tax free—for out-of-pocket medical expenses*

How to Qualify:

You must have a health insurance policy with a deductible of at least $1,500 individual—or $3,000 for families in 2023. Maximum out of pocket: $7,500 for individual; $15,000 for family.

- **Your contribution limit is $3,850 per individual and $7,750 for families (additional $1,000 contribution allowed if you are age 55 for the year)**
- **You can't make HSA contributions after you sign up for Medicare**
- **You can pay Medicare parts B and D and Medicare Advantage with your HSA account—but not Medigap**
- **You can pay a portion of long-term care premiums with your HSA account**

How to Best Utilize:

- **If you are in financial position to do so (**<u>after you have addressed all areas of your finances appropriately</u> **and you have maxed out your 401k at the highest level that is allowed to get your employer match)—let your money in the HSA account grow tax-free and use it only during your elderly years or during your retirement years**

- **Try to pay your current year deductibles and co-payments with your current income or savings**

- **Consider mutual funds and stocks (if your plan allows them in your portfolio) not just savings accounts**

- **Maximize your contribution and think long-term—in 20 years you will be amazed at the growth of the account**

Income Tax

You must look at your current income taxes that you pay on a local, state, and federal level and analyze (or pay a competent professional) them in a thorough manner to see if you can reduce or eliminate the taxes that you pay.

If you currently receive a large refund, you may want to <u>adjust your w-4</u> **(payroll withholding).**

Itemized Deductions

Under the "Pease Limitations" that reduce the value of itemized deductions there would be a limitation on the amount of itemized deductions. Medical, Charitable, Miscellaneous and State and local taxes—among others have limitations.

With updated legislation the limitations are permanently repealed until at least 2025 for many taxpayers.

Mortgage Debt Relief Act

The Consolidated Appropriations Act **(CAA)** was signed into law on December 27, 2020—as a stimulus measure to provide relief to those affected by the pandemic and it **extends the exclusion of cancelled qualified mortgage debt from income for tax years 2021 through 2025**.

However, the maximum amount of excluded forgiven debt is limited to $750,000.

Office in the Home

The home office deduction allows qualified taxpayers to deduct certain home expenses when they file taxes. To claim the home office deduction on their 2021 and later tax return, taxpayers generally must exclusively and regularly use part of their home or a separate structure on their property as their primary place of business.

Be aware of the unwise use of claiming an office in your home as there are caveats and nuances that you want to be aware of prior to claiming this deduction.

Payroll Taxes (Social Security, Medicare & Other Withholdings)

Although your Social Security and Medicare withholdings are mandated by law—you may be able to control other areas of your withholdings.

You control your w-4 withholding—your retirement contributions (if you have an employer who provides a match it may be wise to contribute at a level of the match)—and other withholdings that your employer may offer.

Be sure to consider an IRA—Traditional or Roth. A traditional has the potential to reduce your yearly taxes and help you save for your future. You would be taxed at withdrawal.

A Roth provides no immediate tax reduction—but your contributions and earnings would grow tax-free, and you can withdraw your "contributions tax-free" at basically any time.

With an IRA income limits and other technicalities must be met.

Property Taxes

You must analyze your current property taxes and if you feel they are too high you can utilize the appeal process to possibly get them reduced!

Be sure that you know the property tax amount that you currently pay and be sure that you have properly applied for the homestead exemption and other exemptions that may be available in your community.

*Be sure you know the strength or weakness of your local government, as they possess the power to increase or decrease your future **Millage Rates**—and by knowing the condition of your government you can better plan for the likelihood of tax increases in the future.*

You can possibly find the tax rate in your community or a community that you plan on moving to by searching on local government websites in your area or the area that you plan on moving to.

You can also go to retirementliving.com to get an overview of property and other taxes in your state—or a state that you anticipate moving to.

Always realize that "property taxes" are local in nature—which means they can vary significantly from state to state, county to county or city to city!

Rental

If you have rental properties, you can utilize them to possibly decrease your annual taxes if you file them on schedule E (Rental Property form) or a K-1 partnership tax return.

If you have the property set up under a **schedule C—self-employed form**, you can also possibly utilize the rental properties on your personal tax return to help reduce your taxes owed or increase your refund amount. Rental property deductions and the proper use of depreciation are a few of the major deductions left for the modest income taxpayer.

If your rental properties are "corporately held" you would possibly gain a tax advantage on your corporation's return.

If you had a pass-through corporation (S-corporation) you would possibly have taxable income on your personal tax return. If the S corporation reported a loss, you could possibly reduce the amount of taxes that you owe or increase your refund amount on your personal tax return.

Retirement

It is important that you have a realistic understanding of how your retirement income will be taxed at the state as well as federal level!

You must have a basic understanding (right now) of how your Estate & Inheritance taxes, Social Security Benefits, IRA's, Pensions & Other Retirement Accounts will be taxed during your retirement years.

Taxation of the above are consistent at the federal level—but varies greatly from state to state. Be sure you understand the taxation of your retirement income in your state or the state you plan on moving to during your retirement years!

Do you know if estate and inheritance taxes are applicable in your state based on the size and value of your estate? Do you know whether you are investing in a tax-efficient manner?

Do you know if Social Security benefits will be taxed in your state or the state that you plan on retiring in?

Do you know the states that don't tax income at all (Alaska, Florida, Nevada, South Dakota, Texas, Washington, and Wyoming)?

Do you know if there are exclusions in your state that allows some or all your retirement income to be excluded from taxation?

For example—in Georgia there is a generous retirement income exclusion of $65,000 for taxpayers 65 and older ($130,000 if Married Filing Jointly). Those age 62 to 64 can take a $35,000 exemption per person.

Did you know that 6 States (California, Minnesota, Nebraska, North Dakota, Rhode Island, and Vermont) offer no exclusions at all for retirement income?

In short, it is your responsibility to look into how your taxes will be affected during your retirement years at both the federal, state and possibly local level.

Sale of Residence

The sale of your residence if done properly could lead to a real windfall for you and your family.

If you remain at the residence for 2 plus years and later sell your property at a gain you can exclude $250,000 of the gain if you are single—and up to $500,000 of the gain if you are married.

Be sure you know all of the parameters involved (prior to selling your home) if you are considering selling your home and you want to exclude the gain from taxation.

Note: if a portion of your residence is used for business and deducted on your taxes—that portion will be subject to recapture (will be taxed at time of sale)—thus the amount of your excluded gain will be reduced.

Sales Tax

You must realize that sales taxes are here to stay, and you must be prepared to pay them now and in the future.

Unless you live in Alaska, Delaware, Montana, New Hampshire, or Oregon you will have to pay sales tax on your purchases.

If you travel a lot, be sure that you understand that hotel and lodging taxes vary substantially from state to state—and even city to city—in the same state. You may pay as low as 9.4% in Colorado Springs, Colorado to as high as 17.5% in Birmingham, Alabama. The average rate usually fluctuates in the 13% to 14% range across the United States.

To find the sales tax rate in your state or a state that you plan on moving to or visiting—check with your states government website or the state website that you plan on moving to or visiting.

Stepped-Up Basis

It is important that you understand the concept of "stepped-up basis"—as it simply means that you will get a break on your taxes if you inherit a house, stocks, bonds, mutual funds etcetera—from your parent(s) or spouse due to the value being assessed at the current market price—not the value when it was purchased.

If your parent(s) were to transition and as part of the estate you received a house currently valued at $350,000, but the property was purchased by your parent 30 years ago for $50,000—you would not owe taxes on $300,000 (the difference between purchase price and the current value if you were to sell immediately after your parents transition).

Instead, if you sold the property for $350,000—you would owe zero in taxes.

If you sold the property for $400,000 you would owe taxes of $50,000 ($400,000 minus $350,000)—meaning the value of the property was "stepped-up" to the current market value of $350,000.

That is **important information to know on the front end** whether you are inheriting property or plan on leaving property for your heirs.

It is important to realize that in similar fashion—stocks, bonds and mutual funds also receive "stepped up basis" treatment when they are inherited.

If your parent purchased stocks 20 years ago for $15,000 and at the time of their transition the stocks are worth $200,000—your basis would be stepped-up to $200,000 and if you sold immediately for $200,000, you would owe zero in taxes.

If you sold the stocks 2 years later for $300,000—you would owe taxes on $100,000 ($300,000 minus $200,000) instead of $285,000 ($300,000 minus the $15,000 original basis).

Always realize that inherited IRA's whether ROTH or Traditional can be tricky—as there are certain rules, guidelines and nuances that must be adhered to if your goal is to minimize your taxes.

Be sure to utilize competent professionals if you were to inherit a home, stocks, bonds, mutual funds etcetera—whether inside or outside of a retirement account.

In addition, be aware that if your parent(s) had income (salary, interest, dividends etcetera) that was owed to them at the time of their transition—income tax could still be owed on the income, and you might be required to pay it.

NOTE: Always keep the federal and state exemption amounts in mind when you are receiving or leaving property because of a loved one's transition—or your transition.

Even though you may be eligible for the federal exemption if your estate is smaller than 12.92 million (2023 limit) and possibly double that amount if it was your spouse who transitioned—you may indeed owe at the state level, so always keep that in mind when doing your tax planning.

Tax Preparation

For income tax preparation you can utilize the tax professional of your choice—or if your tax situation is not very complicated you can choose among—the following:

Tax Preparation Page (TheWealthIncreaser.com)

www.HRBlock.com

www.1040Return.com

www.turbotax.intuit.com

www.onepricetaxes.com

CHAPTER 6 Education Planning Basics—What You Must Know About Education Planning

Learn about education planning basics...

Education Planning is an area of financial planning that deserves real attention if you or your family member(s) anticipate improving your (formal) education in the future.

Due to the rising costs and increases above the level of inflation— it is important that you start early, and you have a real plan for success in place prior to establishing your educational funding strategy!

Do you know the steps that you need to take to reach the educational goals for yourself and your family?

Have you even considered the need for educational planning?

And do you know the proper way to implement a plan that will work for you or your family?

In the paragraphs that follow we will address how you can best utilize "education planning" in a manner that serves your and your family's long-term interests!

When Should You Start?

If your goal is to reach your educational goals, you must have a funding plan in place.

The earlier that you start in your life stage—the more effective you will normally be in reaching your targeted amount that is needed for your or your kids educational costs.

Types of Funding Vehicles

There are a **number of ways** that you can save for your and your family's educational goals.

- **Coverdell Education Account**

- **Custodial Accounts**

- **Home Equity/Refinance**

- **IRA's**

- **529 College Savings Plans**

- **Prepaid Tuition Plans**

Other ways to pay for higher education expenses include the following:

- **Employer Provided Assistance**

- **Home Equity/Refinance**

- **Military Assistance**

- **Private Loan**

- **PLUS Loan**

- **Non-Profit Loan**

- **Your Current Income**

Also consider scholarships and other means of paying for your or your child's education. Be sure to utilize the creativity that you have inside your mind and heart to find other ways that you can fund your or your family members educational costs.

Be sure to inspire and motivate your kids to achieve at their highest level—both academically and athletically—as scholarships are available in many forms!

The keys to funding your and your family's educational goals are to start as early as possible, invest consistently and consider increasing the amount if you receive a future raise or other financial windfall.

You must use the "time value of money and compounding" to your and your family's best advantage, and by starting early you can do just that!

What Funding Method Should I Choose?

The funding method that is appropriate for you and your family depends on your current financial situation and your expected educational expenses.

If you have <u>discretionary income</u> at the right level you can utilize a Coverdell Account which gives you more control (you direct your investment choices) than a 529 plan or the others mentioned above—with the possible exception of an IRA.

If you have all areas of your finances addressed appropriately you can possibly (if you or your child qualify) maximize your utilization of an IRA (ROTH) to save for your or your children's educational costs (assumes your retirement funding has been properly addressed by other funding means).

If you expect your funding level to be very high, you may need to use a combination of approaches. A great site for calculating your funding needs and/or forecasting your educational expenses is <u>**FinAid.org**</u>—<u>**The Smart Student Guide to Financial Aid.**</u>

In short, your unique and individual family situation and what you desire in the future education wise for you and/or your family— along with <u>life's uncertainties</u> that you will face—will determine the approach that is best for you and your family.

If you did not put an effective savings plan in place or you had a <u>major life emergency</u> you might have to use a Home Equity/Refinance, Military Assistance, Private Loan, PLUS Loan, Non-Profit Loan, Your Current income—or other <u>creative means</u>

to attain the educational goals that you desire for yourself or your child.

Also, depending on your income there are a number of <u>Federal— and possibly State Financial Aid and Scholarships </u>that may be available that you or your kids may be eligible for.

With many college graduates now entering the workforce with astronomical student loan debt that prevents them from achieving the success that they desire and deserve now commonplace—you want to do all that you can to avoid that unfortunate scenario.

College Savings & Eligibility for Financial Aid—Tips

1) Assess your risk level and know your investment philosophy. Many who save for college costs consider low risk investments as they are easier and less stressful to manage, however they may not give you the 8% or higher return that you will need to fund rising tuition costs.

A common investment mix that many who save for college costs use consists of:

70% High Risk—30% Low Risk from age 1 to age 6

60% High Risk—40% Low Risk from age 7 to age 10

30% High Risk—70% Low Risk from age 11 to age 16

It is also wise to transfer "high risk investments" to "low risk investments" by December 31st of your child's junior year so you won't have to count the "capital gains" as income in the year that you apply for financial aid.

529 and other tax advantaged plans usually do not have a capital gains issue and the fund manager will normally shift funds to more conservative investments as the child ages. With a Coverdell Account and a ROTH IRA, you would have more control over your investment choices—and they have tax advantages as well.

Always realize that you can reduce you credit and financial risk by "choosing an advisor the right way" and "investing in the right manner." Although risk will always remain a part of the human equation—there are things that you can do to reduce your risk—thereby increasing your and your family's opportunity for future success!

Also, consider continuing to invest while your child attends college to reduce or eliminate the amount of borrowing that may be needed. By doing so you will put yourself and your family in position for a more prosperous future.

2) Always realize that "Timing" is crucial when planning for educational costs. The sooner you start and the more time that you have to save, the more effective your investment results will be.

3) Start aggressive in your early years of investing and move to more conservative investments as time goes by. If you save $100 per month for 20 years at 8% return, you could have over $50,000 dollars. If you save $200 per month for 20 years at 8% return—you could have well over $100,000 dollars.

4) Evaluate the best "investment vehicle" for your education funding—529—Coverdell—ROTH IRA—Pre-paid Tuition—or other investment vehicles.

5) Review Your Investment selections on a consistent basis—at least annually. By doing so you can adjust your holdings if need be.

6) Be sure you have a "diversified portfolio" such as stocks, bonds, money market, savings, and other appropriate accounts. By doing so you reduce your risk exposure, and you give yourself the opportunity to have above market returns. Be sure to stay away from investments that you are not comfortable with, and you don't readily understand.

7) Be sure to save consistently such as monthly, quarterly, yearly etcetera—and be sure to consider "dollar cost averaging" where you invest a consistent amount monthly (or other time frame) over several years.

8) Realize that it is normally better to save in "your name" and not your child's name if you are funding your child's education. By doing so you normally increase your odds of obtaining federal aid.

9) Be sure to save in a tax-advantaged way—529 plans are exempt from federal tax and in many states, they are exempt from state tax—as well. Some States also offer a tax deduction on their state tax returns.

If you use a Traditional IRA, you would be taxed on the withdrawal, but you would not be hit with an "early withdrawal penalty"—however, if you saved utilizing a ROTH IRA you could withdraw your "contributions" and "earnings" tax free—if you were to use the funds for higher educational purposes.

If you are over age 59 ½ you would not have an early withdrawal penalty with either IRA, however with a Traditional IRA you would owe taxes on the withdrawal amount—based on your tax bracket.

10) Start transferring from your account several years before your child will begin school to avoid capital gains taxes and your gains being classified as income. By doing so you would normally increase your odds of obtaining federal aid.

By starting early with your savings plan and addressing your finances in a comprehensive manner, you put yourself and your family in a position to attain the success that you and your family deserve!

By "really" applying what you have just learned you can put yourself and your family in "real" position to attain the educational goals that you have always dreamed of for your kids, and you will start on a journey of success that can in many cases go from generation to generation!

CHAPTER 7 Estate Planning/Wills & What You Need to Know

Learn the importance of Understanding the Basics of Estate Planning/Wills...

How do you go about putting an effective plan in place that addresses your estate planning and wills in a comprehensive manner?

It can be done if you have the right approach, and you are properly prepared and dedicated to achieving the success that you know is in your future.

- Starting in 2023, individuals can transfer up to $12.92 million to heirs, during life or at death, without triggering a federal estate-tax bill, up from $12.06 million in 2022.

- Since married couples may share exclusions by electing portability, their combined limits are double, allowing transfers of up to nearly $26 million for 2023, compared to just over $24 million in 2022.

- *After surpassing the exemption amount the rate will be 40%, up from 35% and the exemption amounts are now indexed for inflation.*

There's also a higher annual limit on tax-free gifts in 2023, rising to $17,000 from $16,000.

Most consumers won't have to deal with the complexities of estate taxes—however you should still have an awareness of when it might affect you as your goal should always be to increase your net worth!

All consumers should have a valid will created that addresses their wishes for the transfer of their assets after their transition.

Be sure that you are aware of all the following:

Trusts are also an effective way of protecting your family and planning for the transfer of assets. Utilize highly effective Estate Planning Attorneys if you are at the point where you are considering setting up a Trust as it can be complex and must be set up in the proper manner in order for it to be valid and carry out your intended wishes.

"Properly Titling Your Property" is another way to pass on wealth and assets to your family and loved ones. Be sure to give this area serious consideration, and again be sure to use competent highly effective professionals.

"Stepped-Up Basis" is another area that you should be concerned about as some assets will receive favorable step-up basis treatment and some won't.

In your estate know what the basis of your assets will likely be at the time of your transition and plan your tax strategy now—while you are alive—so that your heirs will have a blueprint of what needs to be done after your transition as the adjustment period can be very difficult.

If an asset receives stepped-up basis treatment—that could mean lower taxes for your heirs in the future. If, on the other hand an asset does not receive stepped-up basis treatment—that could mean higher taxes for your heirs.

Use of Insurance

You can use insurance as a major tool to transfer wealth or increase your savings that you can later pass on to your heirs and can be an effective estate planning tool.

You can use _insurance_ to protect the assets that you have accumulated and pass on the assets and the insurance proceeds in a manner that you choose—while "you" are alive!

* Gifting—you and your spouse can "each" gift up to $17,000 yearly (as of tax year 2023) without incurring any tax consequences. Gifting is often used to reduce an estate for Estate Planning purposes.

A gifting strategy can also be used in education planning. In either case competent legal advice should be obtained.

Also be sure to appropriately consider:

Living Wills/Health Care Directive

Power of Attorney

As a consumer you must put an estate plan and/or will in place that addresses your intentions NOW—while you are of sound mind.

You control the ability to direct the way that your assets and insurance proceeds are disbursed.

Be sure to use the control that you now have to address your concerns now, whether it be for estate planning and wills or any other area of your personal finances!

You don't have to let your state or others determine where the things that you value most end up at!

You can transfer your "net worth" in the manner that you choose if you make the decision to do so—today!

Always keep in mind that Estate Planning and Wills are an area of financial planning that is often not approached in the right manner.

Many people transition unexpectedly and have no Will (intestate) and their property on occasion will revert to the "State" in many instances.

It is crucial that you have a "valid Will" at the very least and if your estate is valued at several hundred thousand or more "Estate Planning" may prove to be an invaluable and wise move on your part.

Below you will find additional areas of concern that you need to consider if you want to improve your family legacy with the use of Estate Planning and Wills.

Be sure to analyze all areas of your finances as they normally have a high correlation to your Estate Planning and Wills.

Your insurance, insurance, investments, taxes, emergency fund, education planning, and retirement planning are all areas that are directly related to Estate Planning/Wills and you need to continuously monitor and improve upon all of those areas of your finances.

Do I Have a Need for Estate Planning & Wills?

Depending on your financial net worth and current cash flow situation you may be in position to have a need for a Will and Estate Planning.

As for your Estate Planning/Wills your options include visiting an attorney and/or going online and utilizing a reputable company to create a will for yourself and your spouse.

If you currently don't feel you have a large enough estate to see an Attorney for Estate Planning because your retirement account and New Worth is quite low, make it a goal to increase both to a high level and consider Estate Planning services in the future.

Be sure that you stay abreast of "life changes" (marriages, divorces, births, deaths etcetera) in your family and be prepared to modify your Will if necessary, so that you will not "invalidate" your Will.

Be aware of how your state laws affect the outcome of your Will(s) if you were to transition unexpectedly.

As a married couple you should know what is included in each Will and you should do your best to honor what is stated in the Will should one of you pass before the other.

If you are married, you will need to create "two Wills" so be prepared to pay twice whether you create your Will at an Attorney's Office, Online, or at your Home.

Final Thoughts on Estate Planning & Wills

Estate Planning & Wills are and area of financial planning where more and more consumers are starting to see the need for.

With the baby boom population now maturing many now understand the need for effective planning better now than in the past. However, it is still an area of financial planning that is often overlooked by many.

Be sure to address this area of your financial planning as it can improve the living conditions for your family for generations. Do not procrastinate as this is an area of financial planning that should be addressed immediately.

Chapter 8   Retirement Planning & What You Need to Know

Learn why it is very important to understand Retirement Planning Basics...

It is important that you understand prior to your retirement that there are things that you must do if you want to enjoy the lifestyle that you desire during your retirement years.

If you see yourself playing golf, purchasing your vacation home, pursuing a topic that has really intrigued you, or volunteering for one of your favorite causes—you must ensure that your retirement accounts are properly funded when you retire so that you can do what you desire during your retirement years.

You must do your planning on the front end if your goal is to really enjoy your retirement years! Many retirees often underestimate the amount of income they will have available or underestimate the amount of expenses that they will have in their retirement years.

Below we will list areas of retirement that have been a problem for many and are areas that you must address prior to your retirement, and then expand on what you can do now to address those areas appropriately!

- *Not budgeting enough for retirement—65%-75% of your current income may not be enough, it depends on your goals*

- *Health Care costs are rising and may be more than you expect*

- You must understand that you will have to pay taxes on your retirement income

- Be sure you understand what you will spend on an annual basis during your retirement years

- Be aware that in many cases you will have to pay taxes on some of your Social Security earnings

- The need to provide income for your spouse if you were to transition unexpectedly

- The need to provide for other family members such as your children and/or parents

BUDGETING:

You must understand that if you plan on golfing, providing perks for your children and grandchildren, traveling abroad or any other goal that you may have, it requires that you accurately calculate the "number" that you need to attain to do just that!

You can't depend on traditional benchmarks; it truly depends on your specific goals that you have for yourself and your family!

If you anticipate that you will need $40,000 per year to do what you enjoy doing during your retirement, you must have a real plan of action to get to that number so that you can have the funds that you need for the time that you expect to be alive after you retire.

If you plan on living for 30 years after you retire, you will need 30 times $40,000 or approximately 1.2 million in your account by the time you retire.

Likewise, if you anticipate that you will need $80,000 per year to live at the level that you desire, you will need 30 times $80,000 or approximately 2.4 million in your account by the time you retire.

Keep in mind that both above figures would be reduced if you were to receive Social Security or Railroad Retirement Benefits.

In that case you would reduce the amount that you would need annually by the amount of Social Security or RRB benefits that you would receive annually.

In the first example if you were to receive $10,000 annually from Social Security and you need $40,000 annually to live at the level that you desire, you would now multiply what you needed at retirement as 30 times $30,000 per year and you would therefore only need approximately $900,000 by the time you retire.

In the second example if you were to receive $20,000 annually from Social Security and you needed $80,000 annually to live at the level that you desire, you would now multiply what you needed at retirement as 30 times $60,000 per year and you would therefore only need approximately 1.8 million by the time you retire.

The above figures are approximations only, as there are more accurate ways to predict your retirement number. The above example is a starting point only.

HEALTH CARE:

It is important that you realize that health care costs for pre-retirees and retirees are in many cases at a high level.

Although you may be able to obtain Medicare at age 65, you will still have to pay Part B Medical insurance of over $100 per month plus an annual deductible. In addition, dental services are not covered as of 2023. If you are age 65 and you receive Medicare your out-of-pocket expenses could still be well over a quarter million dollars!

If you factor LTC (Long-Term Care) insurance into the calculation the figure gets even more absurd.

If you retire at age 62 and live to one-hundred years of age—your health care costs could easily approach a half-million dollars.

Be sure you have realistic projections of your health care costs during your retirement years and be sure you have a plan in place now to meet those rising costs during your retirement years— whether by Medicare or effective planning!

RETIREMENT WITHDRAWALS:

If you withdraw money from a traditional IRA or 401K or certain other retirement accounts, you will have to have a plan of action to pay the taxes on them.

If you were to withdraw money from a tax deferred account during your retirement years, expect to pay taxes at your ordinary income tax rate!

Always realize that you can keep your retirement money in a tax-deferred retirement account until you hit age 73!

If you have qualified ROTH IRA withdrawals, you will pay no tax on withdrawals and earnings during your retirement years—and there are **no mandatory withdrawals.**

Therefore, depending on your unique situation, it may be wise to cash in your bond and certificates of deposits or CD's prior to taking the mandatory withdrawals from your retirement accounts.

You can then go and take withdrawals from your taxable investment accounts to take advantage of capital gains and losses to help reduce or offset your taxes (you can deduct $3,000 per year in capital losses against capital gains and carry forward any remaining losses to future years).

If your traditional IRA did not require mandatory withdrawals—you would now do so if you were at the age (73) where it was required—and finally if you had to have additional money to live at the level that you desire, you would tap into your Roth IRA (keep in mind that there are no mandatory withdrawals with a Roth IRA so you could continue to build wealth in this account if you had no need for the funds).

SPENDING HABITS:

Company perks that you once took for granted may not be available during your retirement years. Your other family members may need you to assist them with their living expenses.

Will you be under-prepared or over-prepared?

Social Security Taxes may apply to you:

Depending on your income and filing status, you may owe taxes on your social security and/or retirement earnings. Therefore, be sure you have an idea of how your tax situation will affect your spending habits during your retirement years—prior to your retirement years.

You can go to ssa.gov/mystatements/ to get an estimate of your Social Security monthly income that you can expect during retirement!

ESTATE PLANNING:

A critical component to protecting your assets. Be sure you have a plan in place to pass down your and your spouse's assets.

Always consider the possible reduction of income due to death or disability.

Never Let Retirement Planning Intimidate You!

Don't let what appears to be complex (saving for your retirement) intimidate you by the vast number of choices that you have.

Quite simply, **start with your 401k or other retirement plan** that is offered and **contribute at least to the match** (you must realize that you may have to contribute more and more (possibly 15% to 20%) to this account depending on what the "retirement number" that you have budgeted for mentioned above is—and your other sources of retirement income.

You must then **reduce or eliminate your debt to an acceptable level, properly establish an emergency fund, save in other tax advantaged accounts that you and/or your spouse are eligible for after that such as HSA's and IRA's**—and then **save outside of your retirement account(s)** if you have the **discretionary income** to do so!

You must always keep your management and other fees to a minimum and you must invest in the most tax-advantaged way.

It is just that simple—however diversification, consistency in approach (you must re-balance at least annually), focus of thought and a real commitment on your part will be necessary even when you hire money management professionals.

WHY YOU MUST EXPECT SUCCESS IN YOUR FUTURE

Did you know that increased expectations require increased effort on your part? It is imperative that you have <u>high standards</u> and you <u>set goals that are meaningful and empowering.</u>

You don't want to go into your retirement years with just enough to pay your monthly bills.

You must raise your expectations of what you expect in your future if you desire success at a higher level!

First and foremost, you must determine your investment style.

Are you more of a risk-taker or are you more risk averse?

You must have a "safe pot" that allows you to meet your minimum monthly bills in your retirement years for your life expectancy!

You already know that the downturn of the markets can and has occurred on numerous occasions and you must have a plan in place that gives you a certain level of return with lower risk—so that you can at least live at a basic level of decency.

You already (or should) know that in Corporate America downsizing continues, outsourcing continues, and future stock returns in many sectors are far riskier due to the management style of those who now run many of the fortune 500 and other publicly traded companies!

You must also have another "riskier pot"—that allows you to take some risks that will allow you to obtain a better rate of return so that you can build your wealth more efficiently!

You could possibly use another pot to enjoy life more abundantly as you enter your golden years.

Even though you will be taking on more risk, you can afford to do so if you have a properly established emergency fund—you have a meaningful understanding and effective management of your credit and finances—and you have your retirement needs covered at a level that allows you to live decently in your retirement years!

Do you have a properly funded emergency fund and have you analyzed all areas of your credit and finances in an appropriate manner? Do you even know all of the areas of your finances that you must address?

Do you know how to invest in a manner that benefits you and your family the most? Since you have gotten to this point in this book you should have a real and practical understanding of what you need to do to achieve major success!

The above questions are basic questions that you not only need to ask yourself, you need to answer them honestly and then take the appropriate steps to enhance your current position in all of the areas mentioned above!

Now is the time that you raise your standards and achieve the success that you not only deserve, but also the success that you should expect to happen—within your own mind!

You must know within your mind that if you do xyz—you will achieve xyz!

Do you now know if that is the case within your mind—currently?

If you don't, you can correct that now by taking action on all that you are learning in this book and taking the necessary steps that are relevant to what you currently desire!

Always realize that you can never eliminate risk—nor can you determine the age at which you will make your transition— however you can adequately plan for and increase your odds to age in a graceful style and in a style that may provide you the "excess" returns that can lead to a more prosperous and rewarding retirement!

However, you must <u>develop the mindset</u> to <u>take action</u> in the right way by preparing your mind with the <u>right knowledge</u>—right **NOW!**

You control the expectations of your future outcomes! Do you expect little of yourself during your retirement years or do you seek to live your retirement in abundance?

The <u>decisions and actions</u> that you take at this time will in large part determine the path that you decide to take!

We are of the opinion that <u>you will achieve untold success in your credit, finance and retirement future</u> and we are certain that you will attain just that by <u>decisively applying</u> what you need to apply on a <u>consistent basis</u> in your life—to make what you desire a reality!

Do you know what your dominant gift in your life is? You must discover your gift and success will ultimately occur.

Even when you can't see the finish line and times will get difficult, you must follow through and feel with your sense's the exuberance of the success that you know will occur in your future.

You must continue your work at a very high level to make what you see and expect a reality!

You must <u>expect to win</u>, success and victory must be in your vision and on your radar!

Now is the time that you <u>stop making excuses</u> if you truly desire to move forward.

You must make your <u>future expectations</u> happen by <u>taking action now</u> so that you can move forward in an efficient manner!

Just as this book and our websites are like a magnet to those who truly desire success (it is no accident that you have purchased this book at this time)—so too can you attract others to your vision!

If your vision is powerful and new others will be attracted to it and they will pursue you and seek to see—the vision that you have already seen!

If you pursue your life purpose (or your God given gift) you must expect success and you must be prepared for what will come when you provide a new light that shines brighter than what others have ever seen!

Once you expect success and you work to make it happen, the time will occur when it is time to display your vision to the world to benefit humanity in a major way.

You must pursue your life purpose and do what needs to be done, whether others are looking or not!

You must know that what you desire will occur because there can be no other outcome! Whether it be improving your credit and finances or achieving your life purpose!

You must create your vision and properly focus on that vision on a consistent basis whether that vision is improving your finances or attaining any other goal that you desire.

Once created—your vision has the potential to lead others to see what you see, however you must put in the work that is necessary to make it happen in real time so that your vision has a "real effect" on people from all walks of life!

If you truly expect success in your future, whether financial or otherwise, this book will go a long way in preparing you for that success—right now!

It is our desire that you expect success in your and your family's future and you now have a real understanding of how you can accomplish those expectations—head on!

What are your expectations for your future? Where are you now being taken? Where do you desire to be in your retirement years?

What are you passionate about currently? Passion alone is not enough, you must also have the proper focus and plan of action if you expect to achieve at a high level!

Do you really know what you want in your life?

These are questions that you must ask yourself and answer appropriately.

Once you know the answers, this book and our websites will provide you much of the knowledge and practical application that you need to know to succeed in your future at a level that is expected—if you desire real success!

You will gain the tools that you need to succeed and you will have a real belief in your mind and heart that you can achieve at a level that you can actually accomplish, and at a level that you will come to expect.

If you decide to apply what you are learning at your highest level and in an appropriate manner you can now do so and based on that decision you should expect nothing less than major success in your and your family's future!

CHAPTER 9 You Can Now Effectively Increase Your Wealth if You Put in The Required Effort

Learn why you must dream big—and then put in the required effort...

It is very important that you make good use of your time and you put in the **required effort** to make what you desire in your future occur for you and your family!

Over the years many clients have asked—what will it take for me to achieve the results that I desire in my future?

My answer has always been that it depends on your current knowledge base—your money management personality and where you are now at in your credit and financial life!

If you have low or negative discretionary income—outstanding credit card debt—and many areas of your finances that need to be addressed, it will take **more effort** on your part than those who are not in that position.

Regardless of where you are now at, **you must come to the realization that it will take effort on your part** if you desire to achieve meaningful and significant goals!

This book is the result of imagining and creating a wealth building book that adds value to your life and a book that was designed to help you unlock and achieve the potential in your life so that success can overflow in your life.

And so that you can have the mental working knowledge that allows you to share that success with your loved ones and others.

The goal of **The Wealth Increaser** is to provide information and advice that will lead to positive results that you can share with others <u>and our goal is to also prepare your mind </u>with what you need to succeed on a consistent basis.

It is important that you realize at the earliest time possible that if your goal is to sincerely increase your wealth in an efficient manner it will take major effort on your part.

It is very important at this time that <u>you make good use of your time </u>and you must put in the <u>required effort</u> if you desire real success in **attaining meaningful goals** in your and your family's future!

You must think, plan, and come up with strategies for your future success that will truly lead to the success that you desire.

What You Must Do Now to Make Your Dreams Come True

You must <u>plan—do—and review</u> if you desire to make your dreams come true!

You must come up with the right strategy that will do what it needs to do in order to help prevent <u>bad things</u> from happening to you.

You must make a difference while you are here on earth and make your life count <u>and truly show your worth!</u>

You <u>must have the mindset</u> that you will put in the **required effort** that is needed so that you can live your future with <u>a high level of persistence</u> and not live your future on the terms of creditors and others who could care less about your existence.

You must grow daily in all areas of your life and improve in your knowledge of your finances and you must know what you can, and need to do to improve your current circumstances.

You must be <u>open to new ideas</u> in the area of personal finance and you must expand your thought horizon exponentially!

It is also important that you expose your mind to a more excellent way of managing your personal finances on a daily basis.

You must listen to, read about and view the best material available around personal finance and choose among the best strategies that you feel will work for you and your family.

Doing all of the above **requires effort** on your part, but it is required if you desire to <u>achieve at a very high level</u> in your and your family's financial future in the times that we now live in!

Putting in the **required effort** means that you will make the best use of your <u>time, commitment, determination, focus</u> and <u>other positive qualities of success</u> on a consistent basis!

Now is the time that you <u>supercharge your mind</u> and use this book and our website to get your financial future right!

Your purchasing of this book may have occurred in order to give you the direction that you may need so that you can succeed at this point in your life.

If you have the potential to succeed you must do so, you can't depend on others to do it for you!

By reading and comprehending this book and utilizing our website(s) in an effective manner you can obtain the **potential to succeed** in all areas of your credit and finances—actually doing so is up to you—<u>your choice</u> and <u>your decision!</u>

If you are serious about your and your family's future, you will not retreat and you will not move in the opposite direction of where you need to go!

You must dig deeper, push harder and reach higher toward the success that you desire <u>at this time in your life!</u>

You must be forthright in your approach, and you must operate with a system that is designed to do what it was intended to do, bring lasting wealth building success to you.

You must also utilize a system that will help you attain the success that you desire in the most efficient and effective manner possible!

You must always realize that when you are empowered to do good and do what is righteous, you should do good and what is righteous!

The Wealth Increaser is designed to lift you up and not tear you down <u>and provide you the ability to reach back</u> and bring up those who may be on the wrong path financially speaking—on the same upward path to success that you now have the <u>opportunity</u> to take!

You can <u>achieve success</u> and be a blessing for others in spite of whether you are now attaining major success or financial difficulty is now occurring in your life.

Regardless of what you are going through or what you have been through, success can now happen for you!

You can be more than an enabler as you can now reach back and help others in an empowering manner, <u>if you first get your house in order</u> appropriately!

<u>This book is for those who want to build from the strong credit and finance foundation that they now have or are willing to learn— and act as a springboard for wealth building achievement at a very high level in today's economy or any economy.</u>

How will you handle adversity that will undoubtedly come your way?

Are you a change agent or are you one who operates in theory only?

When <u>difficult times</u> occur in your life <u>you must get into the habit of taking the right action in real time</u> to make what you really desire occur.

And you must realize upfront that it will take **major effort** on your part to do so!

Passion, commitment, creativity, action, work that empowers others—that is what it will take!

Your <u>ultimate goal</u> should be to have an impact in the lives of others. No one will remember you by what your material possessions are, but they will remember you by the imprint that you made in their life!

Compassion—direction—correction—works on our behalf!

Ponder—examine, observe, analyze—take into account—**and consider whether you really have the effort that is needed within you**—or <u>you are determined to get it</u>—to do what you need to do!

We believe that untold success lies ahead in your credit, finances, and life—for you, your family, and your loved ones if you put in the **required effort** on a consistent basis!

We are of the opinion that your reading of this book today has shown you a highly effective way—and you will not go astray— because you now know that you have the tools that are necessary to make the success that you desire occur—starting today!

Major success for you and your family can now happen and in the end it will be you and your family who will truly win!

You can now **increase your wealth** to the level that is the best that is within you, and you now know what to do comprehensively to reach your goals and make your dreams come true!

Learn the importance of being exposed to the right financial management systems at the right time...

In life we all have unique environments, exposures, experiences and the way that we pursue excellence, and it is important that we learn all that we can from those x-factors so that we can direct our future actions in a manner that is more beneficial for ourselves and those whom we come into contact with.

In the remainder of this chapter we will focus on the importance of why you must be **exposed to financial systems** in general--and **exposed to financial systems** that you can readily learn and apply in your daily life to be more specific--that will truly take you towards your goals that are most significant and meaningful to you and your family—in a very efficient manner.

We all want to do things that bring us joy, however from time to time we must dive into topics that are uncomfortable. For many, personal finance or the management of their finances can be a burdensome or uncomfortable process, however it no longer has to be!

By gaining the right financial knowledge you can cover all of your bases and have a comprehensive approach in the management of your finances that can lead to you building wealth more effectively at the **various stages in your life** so that you can do more of what brings joy into your life.

What you need to know financially

You need to know just <u>what does personal finance entail</u> and how broad or wide a net you must cast as most people have no idea of the magnitude or lack thereof of financial planning in an all-encompassing way.

At a <u>basic level</u> and <u>for starters</u> you need to know your monthly intake and outflow of cash as that is what all of the other areas of your finances will be based on—and will flow from.

In easy-to-understand format, you must know how to:

1) <u>Utilize personal finance statements appropriately</u>

1. Establish a personal **b**udget or cash flow statement at a minimum
2. Create a personal **i**ncome statement
3. Create a personal **b**alance sheet
4. Create a personal **n**et worth statement

2) <u>Gain mastery of how you manage your credit</u>

Negative information must be kept off of your credit report

Utilization of your available credit must be at a reasonable level

Time of open accounts are important

Type of accounts are important

Inquiries must be kept at a reasonable level

3) <u>Comprehensively understand your finances in the following areas</u>

Insurance

Investments

Taxes

Emergency fund

Education planning

Estate Planning/Wills

Retirement planning

By just being **exposed to** the 3 steps above—you are far ahead of the average consumer who for the most part has no real understanding of what personal finance encompasses, let alone the ability to use the knowledge of what personal finance encompasses to their and their family's greater benefit.

You must know the **3 Step Approach** and you already know that a:

1) **b**udget or cash flow statement, **i**ncome statement, **b**alance sheet and **n**et worth statement are something that you need to create at the earliest time possible.

You must have mastery of your credit and know how to use the:

2) **5 credit factors** and wise money management to your and your family's advantage.

You are already very familiar with the importance of, and process of managing your:

3) **i**nsurance, **i**nvestments. **t**axes, **e**mergency fund, **e**ducation planning, **e**state planning/wills and **r**etirement planning at a level that is your absolute best

What you need to do financially

Now that you have knowledge of what you need to know (pun intended) **you must take the right steps** and put into action the results of your cash flow statement or budget at a minimum. Whether you have a monthly surplus or a monthly deficit, <u>you are now in position for more effective planning</u> from this point forward.

If you are comfortable with numbers, you may also want to create an income statement and balance sheet so that you can determine your net worth at this time and improve upon your net worth in the coming years.

The creation of a "properly funded emergency fund" will go a long way in helping you increase your net worth in future years!

You must also gain mastery over how you manage your credit by knowing how to **utilize your knowledge of the 5 credit factors**— as that knowledge can prevent you from getting into a difficult financial hole where climbing out is difficult or highly unlikely (you may need to consider filing bankruptcy as a real option).

Finally, you must know how to select the appropriate insurance products and investment options along with knowing the tax basics and doing, education planning, estate planning and retirement planning in a manner that is more advantageous for you and your family—not creditors or others who have no real concern for your lasting success.

In **Appendix A** you will find a more in-depth sample debt payoff plan.

Appendix A can be invaluable if you decide to create a debt payoff plan yourself or will provide much needed guidance of what to expect if you decide to select a professional financial planner to assist you in your wealth building endeavors.

The importance of reviewing what you do financially

Now that you have a comprehensive overview of your finances and you have been **exposed** to all that you need to know (and do) to work toward making your wealth building goals come true— you "must" be aware of your (and/or your financial planner(s) need to review!

You must review your **personal finance statements**, including your emergency fund to make sure you are adequately protected.

You must review your understanding of the **5 credit factors** so that you can make the right or at a minimum—a good decision as it relates to your use of credit.

You must review your **insurance, investments, taxes, education planning, estate planning/wills, and retirement planning** on a routine basis to see where improvements can be made.

Regardless of your past experiences, the environment in which you grew up in and the positive or negative exposures in your life, you are now in position to change all of that to your advantage— and by being **exposed to personal finance** in a way that you can readily understand and utilize—you are now ready to take your prize.

Use your vision for guidance toward being who you were truly meant to be.

Use your mind and heart for continuous review—so that you can ensure that you do all that you need to do—as you exert increased effort to make your dreams come true!

It is important that you "increase your wealth in a manner that provides clarity" and **exposes your mind and heart to all areas of financial planning** that you need to do throughout your life at the earliest time possible.

By doing so you can get out in front of potential disruptions and proactively plan your future in a manner that is more advantageous for you and your family.

You can put yourself in position where you can live with confidence and the success that you desire will not only occur—it will be expected.

You no longer must approach your financial future with doubt, uncertainty, and a feeling of "can't do"—as by purchasing **The Wealth Increaser**, you have positioned yourself in a major way to make your dreams come true.

All the best because of your willingness to be "exposed to financial systems" that can lead to lasting wealth building success...

Copyright© 2014--2023--TheWealthIncreaser.com--All Rights
Reserved

APPENDIX A: Debt Payoff Plan

This Debt Payoff Plan was prepared for a client by TFA FINANCIAL PLANNING several years ago. Even though clients had very modest income, a debt payoff plan was created that met their goals. It is based off creating a **budget or cash flow statement** only.

A personal income statement, personal balance sheet or personal net worth statement that could have given them even more direction was not created, yet they still were able to obtain significant benefit and financial direction.

However, the concepts and principles that were applied are timeless and can also help you achieve success more efficiently. If your financial situation is more complex or less complex than that in this debt payoff plan—a plan tailored for your unique financial position can be effectively created by you or a financial planning professional.

Always realize that all information obtained from our clients remain confidential. In this sample **debt payoff plan** the names have been changed and other sensitive information has been omitted or removed.

This debt payoff plan was created for a young married couple with a young child (4 years old) and the wife was a stay-at-home mom. Her husband was the only breadwinner at the time.

However, after going over this debt payoff plan, they decided to tighten up their budget (shifted 75% of their miscellaneous spending to debt payoff) and pay off their credit card debt of over $21,000 in a more aggressive manner. And their revised cash flow statement was created where they would pay an additional $300 monthly ($600 total) for 36 months which would lead to the payoff of all their credit card debt.

The credit card pay-off schedule was prepared and looked at from several scenarios, including payment of additional $300.00 per month from their variable miscellaneous spending, which is the option they chose.

The result of choosing to go with the additional $300 per month toward their credit card debt was detailed along with the investment potential of investing over a 30-year period with the money that was going toward the credit card payoff. The potential to have $736,252 in their retirement account (starting 3 years after their credit card payoff) in 30 years assuming a payment of $600 monthly and a compound interest rate of 7% was of great appeal to them.

When combined with their 401k contributions and growth and social security income projections—that provided them even more clarity about where they could go in their future—and particularly during their retirement years as they now had a **realistic retirement number** that they could realistically achieve if they stuck to their investment plan. Their health and life insurance were paid on a pre-tax basis by John, who was the only breadwinner at the time. Their rental insurance was paid on an annual basis with their tax refund that they received annually.

Even though they did not get a "comprehensive financial plan" they still improved the direction in their life, and they began a serious journey toward financial freedom—and you can do the same by making a real commitment toward success at this time.

STATEMENT OF CASH FLOW	John & Jane Sample (Prior to Debt Payoff Schedule)	
Monthly Income		
	Current	**$3,200.00**
Wages, Salary, Tips		
Cash Dividends		
Interest Received		
Social Security Income		
Pension Income		
Rents, Royalties		
Self-employment Income		
Other Income		
Total Monthly Income		**$3,200.00**
Fixed Expenses		
Mortgage Payment or Rent		$900.00
2nd Home Mortgage		
Automobile Note		

Personal Loans	
Credit Cards	**$300.00**
Life Insurance	
Disability Insurance	
Medical Insurance	
Long-Term Care Insurance	
Homeowner's Insurance	
Automobile Insurance	$130.00
Umbrella Liability Insurance	
Federal Income Taxes	$160.00
State Income Taxes	$40.00
FICA	
Real Estate Taxes	
PMI/MIP	
HOA Dues	
Other Taxes	
Savings (Regularly)	
Investments (Regularly)	
Retirement Plan Contributions	

Total Fixed Expenses	**$1,530.00**

Variable Expenses

Electricity	$150.00
Gas	$100.00
Telephone	$95.00
Water	$80.00
Cable TV	$85.00
Maintenance	$0.00
Home Repairs	
Home Improvements	

Food	$400.00
Clothing	
Laundry	$0.00
Child Care	$0.00
Personal Care	
Automobile Gas & Oil	$300.00
Automobile Repairs	
Other Transportation	
Education Expenses	
Entertainment/Dining	
Recreation/Travel	
Club/Association Dues	
Hobbies	
Gifts/Donations	
Unreimbursed Medical	
Dental Expenses	
Eyewear	
Miscellaneous	**$400.00**
Total Variable Expenses	**$1,610.00**

Net Cash Flow

Total Monthly Income	$3,200.00
Total Fixed Expenses	$1,530.00
Total Variable Expenses	$1,610.00

Discretionary Income
(Income - Expenses)   **$60.00**

The credit card pay-off schedule was prepared and included in their updated cash flow statement that include payment of an additional $300.00 per month ($600 total), which was the option they chose.

STATEMENT OF CASH FLOW

John & Jane Sample (After Debt Payoff Schedule)

Monthly Income

	Current
Wages, Salary, Tips	**$3,200.00**
Cash Dividends	
Interest Received	
Social Security Income	
Pension Income	
Rents, Royalties	
Self-employment Income	
Other Income	

Total Monthly Income	**$3,200.00**

Fixed Expenses

Mortgage Payment or Rent	$900.00
2nd Home Mortgage	
Automobile Note	
Personal Loans	
Credit Cards	**$600.00**
Life Insurance	
Disability Insurance	
Medical Insurance	
Long-Term Care Insurance	
Homeowner's Insurance	
Automobile Insurance	$130.00
Umbrella Liability Insurance	
Federal Income Taxes	$160.00
State Income Taxes	$40.00
FICA	

Real Estate Taxes
PMI/MIP
HOA Dues
Other Taxes
Savings (Regularly)
Investments (Regularly)
Retirement Plan
Contributions

Total Fixed Expenses   **$1,830.00**

Variable Expenses

Electricity	$150.00
Gas	$100.00
Telephone	$95.00
Water	$80.00
Cable TV	$85.00
Maintenance	$0.00
Home Repairs	
Home Improvements	
Food	$400.00
Clothing	
Laundry	$0.00
Child Care	$0.00
Personal Care	
Automobile Gas & Oil	$300.00
Automobile Repairs	
Other Transportation	
Education Expenses	
Entertainment/Dining	
Recreation/Travel	
Club/Association Dues	
Hobbies	

Gifts/Donations
Unreimbursed Medical
Dental Expenses
Eyewear
Miscellaneous $100.00

Total Variable Expenses   **$1,310.00**

Net Cash Flow
Total Monthly Income $3,200.00
Total Fixed Expenses $1,830.00
Total Variable Expenses $1,310.00

Discretionary Income
(Income - Expenses)   **$60.00**

How to Prepare Your Monthly Budget

Monthly Expenditure
___

Auto loan payment	$_____
Auto maintenance	$_____
Childcare	$_____
Clothing	$_____
Contributions	$_____
Credit card pmts.	$_____
Dues	$_____
Entertainment	$_____
Food	$_____
Household maint.	$_____
Income & SS taxes	$_____
Insurance	$_____
Personal care	$_____

Property taxes	$_____
Rent payment	$_____
Mortgage payment	$_____
Retirement Invest.	$_____
Saving/investing	$_____
Transportation	$_____
Utilities	$_____
Other	$_____
Auto loan payment	$_____
Auto loan payment	$_____
Auto loan payment	$_____
TOTAL Monthly Expenditures	$_____

Monthly Receipts

Wages	$_____
Dividends	$_____
Interest	$_____
Rental	$_____
Royalty	$_____
Other	$_____
TOTAL Monthly Receipts	$_____

Net Cash Flow

Total monthly receipts		$_____
Total monthly expenditures	-	$_____

Monthly Net Cash Flow

$_____

Note: By gathering all your financial data and plugging the numbers into the monthly budget or monthly cash flow statement above, you can see where you now stand financially. By doing so you can plan your future in a more rewarding way and make the achievement of your wealth building goals more attainable so that you can live out the life that you truly desire.

Be sure your income and expenses are as accurate as possible when you plug in the numbers.

Also note that in the above example their discretionary income remained at $60 per month, meaning they are tightening up their monthly spending by reducing their miscellaneous expenses from $400 per month to $100 per month for 36 months.

And thereafter investing the $600 debt payment in their retirement accounts for 30 years after the credit card payoff.

The above debt payoff plan does not consider pay raises and other sources of income that may be available in future years, including the possibility that the spouse will begin working once their child starts attending school full-time or gaining additional income whether through Uber, Lyft, Grubhub and other new economy independent contractor or employment options.

Debt Payoff Synopsis (Provided to Client)

John and Jane, if you put this plan off, not only will you lose a possible $736,252 in future wealth, but you will be giving away thousands of dollars per year in interest each year you delay!

Do you really have money to give away?

By seriously implementing this plan you can begin on a journey that can lead to you pursuing your other goals and objectives that you and Jane outlined in this plan.

Once you clear your credit card debt you will have an extra $600.00 per month that you can use to enhance your emergency fund, save for college, use for entertainment purposes, invest both inside and outside of your retirement plan or pursue other goals that are dear to your heart.

More importantly, you can live your life in a manner where your stress level is reduced and other goals that you have in mind will be more attainable based on your **discretionary income of $600.00 per month that will be created** by the payoff of your credit card debt in 36 months.

Keep in mind the fact that the additional $600.00 per month does not consider salary increases and bonuses or other additional source(s) of income that you and/or your spouse will receive in the future.

The $400 per month that you now spend on miscellaneous activities will be reduced to $100 per month which will give you an additional $300 per month to add to the $300 credit card payment that you are now making so that you can pay off your credit card debt of $21,000 over the next three years.

The above numbers are based on the information that you provided; therefore, the accuracy or lack thereof will vary if the numbers that you provided are not accurate.

All the information that you provided will remain confidential and will not be disclosed to anyone unless required by law.

Other than your name and address, no other information such as account numbers, social security numbers, date of birth or any other specific information that can be used to identify you will be retained by our office.

All the best towards your future success...

Thomas (TJ) Underwood

Appendix B: AXIOMS for Success by Thomas (TJ) Underwood

INCLUDED AS AN ADDED BONUS ARE 30 ORIGINAL AXIOMS DESIGNED TO ENCOURAGE AND INSPIRE YOU TOWARD YOUR FUTURE GOALS IN AN EMPOWERING MANNER:

1) Start strong, cultivate habits of success, move forward—maturity is knowing when to stop foolish behavior

2) You must look forward toward success and settle for nothing less!

You must now give it your best go so that the results that you desire will show!

You must really go after your credit and financial goals this round—and not be deterred by obstacles or roadblocks that slow others down.

You now have or you soon will have all that it takes inside of you to navigate your way forward and make your dreams come true!

Success is now on the way because you have made the decision to read this book today!

3) You must at this time live your life daily knowing with certainty that any **obstacle** that comes your way will not affect your plans—or cause a major delay—in any way!

Now is the time that you do what you need to do and now is the time that you learn something new!

By doing so, you can equip your mind properly and **overcome any obstacle** that you are facing or that you may face—and make your dreams occur at a faster pace!

4) If you believe success lives in you—success will believe in you. You must feel **worthy** of all the **success that is in your future.**

When proper preparation, know-how, execution and faith meet inside of your mind and heart—"success" will say—WELCOME!

5) Always remember that you have the "power" to take your mind to a "good place"—you don't have to stay in a "low place"—if you make the choice not too.

In short, you are worthy of whatever you decide in your mind, that you are worthy of!

6) Always remember that many can quote wise thoughts, very few can apply wise thoughts effectively and in a manner that can transform their life.

You can aim high or aim low—no one else can control your aim—you control how you feel about yourself and the direction that your life will take!

Use that knowledge to control your future and stop blaming others or let how others look at you and feel about you affect your life in a detrimental way!

Use that knowledge to free your mind from anything in your past or your family's past that may be holding you back from reaching your goals!

You have the mental capacity to do great things in your life—you don't have to live your life in strife!

7) Greatness is In You (Give it Your All)

No one can see what you see or do what you do.

You are a unique creation—the world is waiting on you!

Your gifts and talents can be seen all around.

Please don't let us down!

We want to ensure that your gifts are around.

Will you do (be) all that you can—and not let us down!

Your gifts and talents are our reward.

For you not to give it your all, would not lead us forward.

Use your creativity and not negativity—you'll receive a positive charge—and go down in history—as large.

Is it any wonder that you have what it takes?

You can be all that you want to be if you don't put on the brakes!

Do you know that you are great?

Provide us your gift (purpose) for being here—the world can no longer wait!

Do you know that you have the strength that you need—to succeed?

Greatness is in you—you can make all your dreams come true!

Starting today—will you do what you need to do?

8) You must realize that hope, wishful thinking or prayer—without action is not a strategy and you must know that major success can be in your and your family's future <u>by taking appropriate action</u> and doing what you need to do—on a consistent basis!

Putting a <u>plan in action</u> that is measurable and has definite deadlines for achievement is a strategy—if done properly!

9) You can <u>demonstrate faith</u> and the fact that you value your and your family's future by <u>taking action at a high level</u> and <u>achieving at a high level</u>—right now!

You and your family are **worthy** of a prosperous and successful future—now is the time that you affirm that reality!

10) By having faith that you can achieve your goals you can change your life and the direction that you are going—right now!

The key to your success is not the knowledge that you will gain— but how you "comprehend" and "utilize the knowledge" that you will gain—in your daily life.

While learning something new—it is important that you engage your heart and mind at your highest level, and you use your willpower to take the appropriate action that you need to take on a consistent basis.

11) Use your imagination and say to yourself—why not me—you should be saying why not me—if there is something big in your future that you really want to see become a reality!

You must realize that you can't wait on others to tell you that it is OK to create what you desire in your future!

12) By being original—thoughts at a high level will be in your midst on a consistent basis and if you act on those thoughts in a meaningful way, you can take your life in the direction of your life purpose.

13) It is important that you act on inspiration that comes from within when it is in your best interest to do so. And you must feel that you are **worthy** of the success that you desire, regardless of the area that you decide to excel in.

14) *Do you know that you are worthy of whatever you think you are worthy of?*

Do you know your purpose for your life at this time?

Answer the right questions appropriately—and use the knowledge that you will learn daily to reach your highest heights as you move towards the success that you desire for yourself and your family!

15) You must be diligent in your approach as well as vigilant in your approach and you must be fully committed to achieving your goals at this time!

You can excel—you can come up and out of any situation that you are in if you have the proper mindset! You must be excellent in spirit and always move forward—**mediocre goals must not be a part of your mindset.**

16) **If you diligently work toward your goals and you do not let distractions negatively affect you—you will gradually improve and success will occur if you are consistent in your approach towards working toward your goal(s)!**

17) Pursuing excellence (winning) requires focus of thought and the decision by you to operate in excellence! It is the intentional use of your mind to enhance the probability of the outcome that you desire.

18) You must have positive thoughts, you must believe in yourself at a very high level, you must get back up and make the best of your situation—NOW!

You must excel, you must move forward, you must focus daily, you must get better—you must pay attention to the details!

You must **plan for your success...**

19) *Whether you know it or not it is your responsibility to transform your mindset and take the necessary actions that are needed to ensure a prosperous and productive future for you and your family!*

20) *You must <u>pursue excellence!</u> You must not only possess the knowledge that you will gain in your mind, you must also comprehend and use that knowledge on a constant basis if you are to attain true success!*

You must do a detailed analysis of your <u>"mental thought process"</u> and then make the decision to improve in areas that you are weak or deficient in.

You must do a sincere and honest self-analysis within "your mind" and you must realize up-front that it will take <u>constant effort</u> on your part to <u>cultivate the habits</u> that are needed for success.

21) You must have <u>self-confidence</u> and <u>self-discipline</u> at all times and you must let the enthusiasm or excitement that you now have on the inside of you grow in an ever-increasing manner!

By doing so in a <u>sincere manner</u> you can put yourself in position for a **<u>winning future</u>** where you are in control and the success that you desire is the ultimate outcome.

22) You must know what you need to do at all times when it comes to managing and improving your credit and finances and, in this MILLENNIUM, —it is more important than ever that you get it right on the front end.

You must make it a priority to gain the "mental working knowledge" that is needed on a daily basis to attain <u>success</u> at a high level.

By doing so you will know how to avoid bad decisions that consumers make on a constant basis without even realizing they are making a bad decision!

23) You must understand that if you gain the **<u>proper preparation</u>** and the **<u>proper knowledge</u>** on the front end, you gain the insight that is **<u>essential for success</u>** in today's economy!

You don't have to let <u>anxiety and uncertainty</u> rule your life and by preparing properly you can avoid financial strife!

24) You now know that Disposable Income **differs** from Discretionary Income.

It is important that you distinguish in your mind that disposable income is money that you have left after paying your taxes—while discretionary income is money you have left over after paying your taxes "and" mortgage/rent, food, utilities, and life's other necessities.

Discretionary Income is money that you can spend or save at your discretion!

25) Did you know that you can increase your income by <u>**making compound interest work for you**</u> and not against you?

By understanding and being able to distinguish among the various types of income and understanding how compounding works—you put yourself in position to understand your personal finances in a more meaningful and effective manner!

You also put yourself in position to where you can control your future in a more <u>"financially alert manner"</u> and in a manner that will lead to true success for you and your family!

26) Always remember, that a high level of **dedication** will lead to a high level of results when you are pursuing your credit, finance or any other goal or objective that you may have!

<u>**You achieve more when you set goals—limitless and largely untapped areas of accomplishment can occur—if you remove limitations from your mind and you set meaningful goals!**</u>

27) You must understand that it is difficult to do what needs to be done on a daily, weekly, and monthly basis to improve your finances to a high level. However, by applying the right knowledge you can gain the mental fortitude that you need—to succeed!

28) You must get to a point where you can set a goal—no matter how small—and actually pursue and achieve that goal.

That will then give you the confidence that you need and if you continue to set and reach your goals consistently, you will develop the **habit of self-discipline** that is required in your financial and other areas of your life.

You will then have the real belief that you can achieve your retirement goals, pay off your debt in a timely manner, save for your children's education in an efficient manner or reach any other goal or objective that you may have for yourself and your family.

29) You must pursue your credit and financial goals with the real expectation that the goals that you seek in your credit and financial life will "really occur" in your life!

You must pursue your credit and financial goals with real passion, you must really want to achieve the goals that you set deep down in your heart (your intellect, will and emotions must really be involved at a high level) after you have given serious thought to the goals that you want to achieve!

When you are operating in a sincere manner you can more effectively direct your future!

30) When you are operating with "true sincerity" towards your credit and financial goals you can see the vision (your goals) occurring and you can feel it happening.

You have no doubt that what you are seeking will really occur because you are pursuing your goals at such a high level and you have the preparation and knowledge that is necessary that success is the only outcome that is possible!

You cannot deceive yourself; you must pursue your goals with a very high belief that the goals that you seek—will occur!

Appendix C: Thomas (TJ) Underwood—*Real Estate Broker, Financial Planner, Author, Blogger*

Currently **The Real Estate & Finance 360 Degrees Series of Books©** *consist of:*

Book 1) Managing & Improving Your Credit & Finances for this Millennium Paperback **Copyright© 2012**

Book 2) HOME BUYER 411 *The Smart Guide to Buying Your Home* E-book **Copyright© 2014, 2023** Hardback **Copyright© 2023**

Book 3) HOME SELLER 411 *The Smart Guide to Selling Your Home* E-book **Copyright© 2014,2023,** Hardback **Copyright© 2023**

Book 4) The Wealth Increaser E-book **Copyright© 2014, 2023** Paperback **Copyright© 2023** Hardback **Copyright© 2023**

Book 5) The 3 Step Structured Approach to Managing Your Credit & Finances E-book **Copyright© 2014, 2023** Hardback **Copyright© 2023**

Book 6) The FIZBO Manual (For Sale By Owner Guide) E-book **Copyright© 2014, 2023** Hardback **Copyright© 2023**

Book 7) 1-2-3 Credit & Me E-book **Copyright© 2021, 2023** Paperback **Copyright© 2023,** Hardback **Copyright© 2023**

Book 8) Credit & Finance Improvement Made Easy E-book **Copyright© 2014, 2023** Paperback **Copyright© 2023**

In addition, you can find helpful articles on several credit and finance topics by visiting the following websites:

www.the-best-atlanta-real-estate-advice.com

www.realty1sa.com

www.TheWealthIncreaser.com

I welcome your success stories and the positive effect that the books in the series along with the articles on the websites above have had on your life.

All the best...

Copyright© 2014, 2023

Publisher: TFA Financial Planning

Email: tj@TheWealthIncreaser.com

ISBN: 978-1-953994-12-7

The Wealth Increaser will help you:

- Manage your finances effectively throughout your lifetime so that you can realistically determine where you can go financially

- Take charge of your finances in a way that puts you in control and keeps you in control so that you can build wealth more effectively

- Change your life in a major way by providing you a way to achieve major success in clear terms by providing you effective goal setting tips and ways to manage your finances better at the various stages of your life

Thomas (TJ) Underwood is the Real Estate Broker at Realty 1 Strategic Advisors, LLC one of the most successful real estate and financial planning companies in the metropolitan Atlanta area. Realty 1 Strategic Advisors is based in Peachtree City, GA.

He is a former fee-only financial planner and top producing loan processor, and he has assisted clients from as far away as Germany with their financial concerns. The concepts in **The Wealth Increaser** have been utilized by savvy money managers to enhance the likelihood of successfully managing their finances and achieving many of their most significant goals at the various stages of their life.

He is also the creator of **TheWealthIncreaser.com**, one of the leading financial blog sites that can be found in the internet universe.

www.ingramcontent.com/pod-product-compliance
Lightning Source LLC
Chambersburg PA
CBHW060053100426

42742CB00014B/2809